THE
ROAR
OF THE
SEA

CAPTAIN WILLIAM A. CROWELL

AND FRANK CROWELL LEAMAN

BOULDER
PUBLICATIONS

This book is dedicated to my wife, Florence, my children, and my grandchildren.

—Frank Crowell Leaman

Library and Archives Canada Cataloguing in Publication

Crowell, William, 1879-1959, author
    The roar of the sea / William Crowell & Frank Leaman

ISBN 978-1-927099-44-5 (pbk.)

    1. Crowell, William. 2. Voyages around the world. 3. Ocean travel. 4. Sailors--Nova Scotia--Biography. I. Lawlor, Allison, 1971-, author II. Title.

G440.C867L42 2015   910.4'1   C2015-902009-3

Published by Boulder Publications
Portugal Cove-St. Philip's, Newfoundland and Labrador
www.boulderpublications.ca

© 2015 Frank Leaman

Editors: Allison Lawlor, Stephanie Porter
Copy editor: Iona Bulgin
Design and layout: John Andrews

Printed in Canada

 We acknowledge the financial support of the Government of Newfoundland and Labrador through the Department of Tourism, Culture and Recreation.

 Canada Council Conseil des arts   We acknowledge the financial support for our publishing
for the Arts   du Canada   program by the Government of Canada, including the Canada
Council for the Arts, and the Department of Canadian Heritage through the Canada Book Fund.

CONTENTS

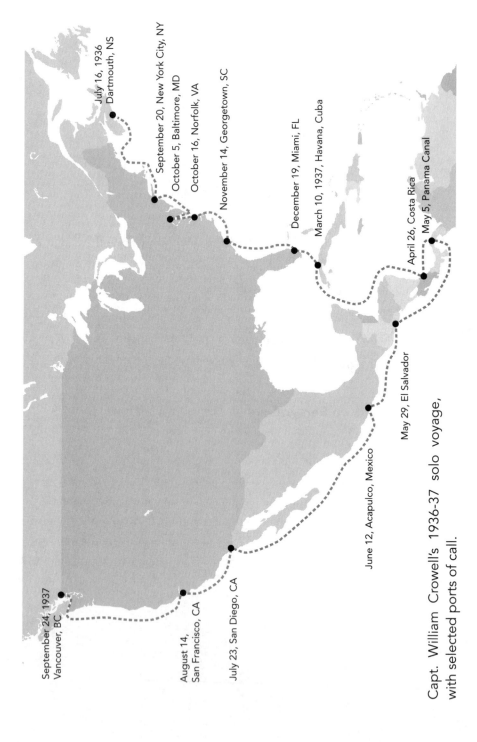

July 16, 1936
Dartmouth, NS

September 20, New York City, NY

October 5, Baltimore, MD

October 16, Norfolk, VA

November 14, Georgetown, SC

December 19, Miami, FL

March 10, 1937, Havana, Cuba

April 26, Costa Rica

May 5, Panama Canal

May 29, El Salvador

June 12, Acapulco, Mexico

July 23, San Diego, CA

August 14, San Francisco, CA

September 24, 1937 Vancouver, BC

Capt. William Crowell's 1936-37 solo voyage, with selected ports of call.

INTRODUCTION

Sitting in the deckhouse of an old trading schooner not far from Halifax harbour, I imagine I can hear the creak of her timbers, the flapping of her sails, the crying of gulls, and the sea splashing against her hull. My imagination takes me to unnamed places. When I return to my surroundings, I look over and see a familiar photograph of my grandfather, Captain William Crowell.

I'm sitting in a replica of an old ship near an exhibit dedicated to solo sailors like my mother's father. Housed in Halifax's Maritime Museum of the Atlantic, the "Days of Sail" exhibit celebrates the courage and spirit of adventure of these men.

Almost 80 years ago, my grandfather set off on an epic voyage that would test his seamanship and his inner fortitude. In July 1936, he sailed from Halifax in the *Queen Mary*, the 23-foot ketch he had built in his simple backyard boatyard, with the goal of reaching Vancouver via the Panama Canal. He did it. The *Queen Mary* was little more than a lifeboat, with a tiny crawl space to protect him from the elements. His only companion was his beloved dog, Togo. On unfamiliar coasts with no radio, no GPS, and no radar to warn of larger ships or pending storms, it took nerves of steel to survive those 14 months at sea.

My grandfather's story is more than a tale of one man's battles on the sea. Certainly, he could recite an exciting sea yarn, but his story is also about the inner battles fought when the storms of life come aboard your boat. The greatest literature, music, and sacred texts all, to some extent, ponder and celebrate the inner strength the courageous exhibit when faced with adversity. Whether it is the death of a loved one, the loss of a job, or a severe injury, a personal upset attacks an individual in much the same way that a storm does a boat at sea. Winston Churchill's famous words "Never, never, never give up" or American author Louis L'Amour's popular wisdom "There will come a time when you believe everything is finished; that will be the beginning" remind me of my grandfather's stoicism. Like so many sailors of his time, he bravely faced the many challenges in his life head-on.

The quality I admired most in my grandfather was his pluck. Even today, long after his death, he gives me strength. When I feel sorry for myself or experience doubt, I hear his voice saying "Be a man." These words make me stand a little taller, knowing that he lived by them. My grandfather had no choice but to be strong. Giving up wasn't an option.

In 1954, almost 20 years after my grandfather returned home from his epic voyage, we gathered his memories and memorabilia in the living room of his Dartmouth home and prepared to write down his story. I had just finished Grade 6. My grandfather, who had only a Grade 3 formal education—though he never stopped reading throughout his life—saw me as educated. Over the next year, I sat with my scribbler and carpenter's pencil, listening to his tales and furiously writing down every word. My grandfather did not rely entirely on memory; he had a logbook from his journey. He had filled its pages with an account of the places, people, and natural wonders he passed along the way. Some of the logbook's pages were so stained with sea or rainwater that they had to be close-hauled, in sailor's lingo, to be read.

The back of the logbook is filled with dozens of signatures and comments in various languages from the people he met. I loved to flip through the pages and trace my finger over the signatures of well-wishers from far-off places like Managua, Nicaragua, or Xcalak, Mexico. I often wondered what these people thought when they met my grandfather in 1936, just before the world slipped into the chaos of World War II.

fog all day and very thick in the harbor the first to meet me was the Mrs bar and welcome me to the City of Vancouver And so end the long voyage of 14 months & 7 days

how dark the night how light the sea as the bark alone

Dear readers many question has been asked me of whales and sharks and aeroplane and in sailing along in such a small boat was I not afraid. in these lines you will probably get some ideas of the ship or just a little bit of excerent on the Golf cost while trying to avoied a large Sperm Cachalot whale it was a fine afternoon with a little fog some time would blow in thick and then the sun would brake up again. given many slowly reaching in on the cost with a light Breas S. quite a few whales had been spoten around the last few days and many schools of whale herin near the cost. I had been catching a few winks of sleep as my dog kept a fearly good look out while strapled in the compass when presentely he rared and berked

A page from Capt. Crowell's logbook.

I can still picture myself, 12 years old, sitting on the 1940s light grey horsehair sofa in my grandparents' living room. I tried to write as quickly as my grandfather spoke, the Westminster Abbey chimes from the gold-faced clock nearby marking the hours. In front of me, a Persian carpet covered the floor and a piano with finely carved legs sat in the corner. My grandfather kept a large framed picture of Togo on the living room wall. For the 12 years of Togo's life they shared a special bond. The dog's love, bravery, and loyalty made my grandfather's 1936 voyage possible. He told me many times that if he had lost Togo overboard, he would have abandoned his trip.

My grandfather could roar like a lion; he projected a strength that always made me feel safe. He told me tales of shipwrecks, sailors from faraway places, whales, square-riggers, and U-boats—and I was as spellbound as if the stories were unfolding out of *Treasure Island*. Occasionally he would jump out of his seat and gesture an action, maybe a fist fight or a struggle with a whale. He never failed to deliver the unexpected. I guess that's what kept me there on summer days, even when I wanted to play outdoors with my friends. When we were finished, he took my handwritten pages and paid someone to type them—I could write, but I couldn't type.

I still wonder what drove him to undertake his dangerous sea voyage. A letter I found in my grandfather's logbook written to my grandmother, Elizabeth, after he arrived in Vancouver in 1937 revealed the depth of his conflict. He reminisced about his time with her and asked why—since he loved her and their only daughter (my mother)—would he leave for a year and half and subject himself to such a difficult and lonely trip? The letter is filled with confusion and guilt.

A poet friend once asked me to consider the conflicting elements in a sailor's life, how it must be difficult to reconcile a life at sea with a life at home. "Would it have been possible for your grandfather to sail away if he hadn't had someone waiting for him at home, someone who anchored him?" I don't know the answer. I know of men who gave up the sea after losing their lifelong mate. An Acadian fisherman once shared an old saying that may explain some of my grandfather's restlessness: "When we're at sea, we want to be on land; when we're on land, we want to be at sea."

I know my grandfather was restless, but still I can't answer these simple questions: Why did he do the trip? And why record it? What ghosts called him to ask me to write down his story? Did he seek personal recognition or simply someone who would listen?

My grandfather's character was tested on the ocean. The ocean, however, has never tested mine; for me, it represents spiritual peace. When I seek help or guidance, I go to Lawrencetown Beach, a popular sand and cobble shore near Dartmouth, and look out at the ocean. I usually find serenity there. Maybe it was the same with my grandfather. He never told me.

I've tried to imagine what it would have been like to be alone off the coast of Mexico or Central America in 1936, with no GPS or marked buoys as navigational aids, and unable to speak Spanish. The world was close to the brink of war: plans to blow up a lock in the Panama Canal were thwarted, and U-boat traffic posed unseen dangers. It was a dangerous time to travel along thousands of miles of coastline, bays, and rivers. My grandfather was clearly not seeking comfort or security when he decided to sail into this boiling cauldron of uncertainty. A patriotic man, he had worked briefly with the military and the police in his early career, and he received help from the British Consulate at various stops during his travels. On his long solo journey, he carried a shotgun for protection, but I'm not sure if he ever used it.

In 1975, I travelled to Roatán, Honduras, so that I could see for myself at least one of the places my grandfather had visited four decades earlier. Located between the islands of Útila and Guanaja, Roatán is the largest of the Honduras Bay Islands. Formerly known as Ruatan or Rattan, the island is located near the Mesoamerican Barrier Reef, the largest barrier reef in the Caribbean Sea (the second largest in the world after Australia's Great Barrier Reef). In 2015, the island is a much sought-after stop for cruise ships and divers; tourism and fishing are the island's most important industries. But when I arrived in Roatán in the mid-1970s, the island was dotted with primitive huts on stilts. There were no tourists. During my two weeks there, countless children begged me for money and food. Soldiers were everywhere. It was the same year as the Honduran *coup d'état*, when Oswaldo López Arellano was ousted by General Juan Alberto Melgar Castro.

I imagined my grandfather sailing along this wild, dangerous coast dotted with reefs, beset by unpredictable weather and political uncertainty. I spotted boat wrecks along the coastline and was grateful that the *Queen Mary* hadn't suffered the same fate.

It's time to let my grandfather tell his story.

—Frank Crowell Leaman

THE ROAR OF THE SEA

My grandfather, a sea captain, lived his retired days with our family in a little cottage in Three Fathom Harbour, a fishing community east of Halifax. I remember his stories vividly; they sank deeply into my young mind. From his boyhood through his working years, my grandfather knew no other home but the decks of Nova Scotia-built ships. My father's early life, too, was spent on the sea and in shipbuilding. I carried on in their footsteps.

Capt. William Crowell.

My ancestors left to us the world's greatest industry, the shipbuilding trade. These great masters, with their courage and love of the sea, pioneered the sea lanes to foreign lands and built this great world. On the decks of Nova Scotia-built ships, they trimmed their white sails, carrying the flag of Nova Scotia to the four corners of the world. It was a time of wooden ships and iron men, now only a memory in books on library shelves or in the homes of some almost forgotten sons.

This book is the life of one ordinary seaman. What I write is true. It may not be as harmonious or amusing as the stories of Sam Slick, the character created by Thomas Chandler Haliburton, but these are my stories—stories from my life.

CHILDHOOD

I will go back to my childhood days and the cottage, the home of my father. During the last years of my grandfather's life, he spent several winters in our small home. I remember his chair in the kitchen, the Waterloo stove, the stories he told, and the songs he sang. How I loved that grand man of the sea. As I grew up, between the ages of five and 12, he would stroll with me across the fields or by the lake shore or accompany me out in the boat with a fishing line.

So gentle were his ways—so different from the many seagoing types that I joined in later years. Till he retired, he spent his life on the decks of large square-rigged ships. The decks of these ships were his home; he had no other.

> *Oh, how I recall that voice again*
> *   The one I loved so dear,*
> *I knew no one so good and true*
> *   With him I had no fear.*
> *As I strolled with him through trees or field,*
> *   Sometimes upon his arm,*
> *He taught me prayers, he sang me songs,*
> *   He told me right from wrong.*
> *He said to me, "You are my boy,*
> *   "My ship and all its stores,*
> *"And that old sea chest that has long been mine,*
> *   "Someday it will be yours."*

My dear grandfather, his sea chest, his sea stories, and his songs live in my memory. He would open up that chest and go over everything, the many beautiful things, and fold them and place them carefully back in the box after telling us about them. Looking inside the box, I'd see a ship in a bottle, a lighthouse, and water paintings decorating the four sides of the box. On the inside cover was a painting of a small square-rigged ship called *The Golden Gate*. How real it looked, with her British flag and her numbers in flags. With his trembling hand, my grandfather would add pictures of ships under sail and at anchor on the box's cover. He must have been an artist of no mean ability in his early life.

During the winter of my 14th year my grandfather became confined to the house, and in early May I became heir to that chest and his belongings. Under his pillow was a letter addressed to "My Dear Boy." I did not have to open it to know it was mine.

> *Oh, could I lock this worried mind*
> *And find my past untrue,*
> *And wake up in the early morning,*
> *And start the day anew.*

My grandmother—my father's mother—had incredible strength and an equally incredible temper. At age 50 she fell from an ox cart, and the wheel went over her body and fractured her hip. For two years, she was unable to walk and, afterward, she walked with a stick. But she weathered the gale and, for 45 more years, visited the neighbourhood as a midwife, paying six visits to our home.

I remember her visits; she would arrive at our home by ox cart or horse and sleigh, according to the season. She was not very friendly to me or to any of the family. She had the voice of a bull moose and the temper of an evil spirit. Our family was always glad to see her return home. My father was a very gentle and mild man, and I often wondered how he could be so different from his mother.

Our little cottage was by the side of a lake where I learned to fish, row, and swim. One day, when I was four years old, neighbours gave me a little black and tan pup, which I named Frisk. As he grew older, Frisk followed me everywhere. For the 13 years he lived, he was all mine. Our barnyard stock consisted of a pig, a few hens, an ox, a cow, and Frisk. If I remember rightly, we once had four sheep too. Food was hard to get and meals were not regular. On the days my grandmother was with us she did the work around the house, with the help of my eldest sister. She looked after the straining of the milk and churned on Saturday mornings. The churn had a hand plunger.

I was perhaps eight years old on my grandmother's last visit. On that particular Saturday morning she had poured the cream into the churn, but had left it to go out to the clothesline. The churn was open, so Cliff, my brother, and I thought we would sample a few spoonfuls while her back was turned. Frisk jumped up on the table to be near me. When we heard my grandmother's stick on the porch, we made a clean getaway. Frisk was not so fortunate. Somehow he got turned around, head-up, his nose just out of the churn and as pretty a cream colour as could be. We feared something terrible might happen to him, but my grandmother simply plucked him out of the churn, and he made a quick retreat. That was not the end, however—I was the one upon whom she wreaked her anger.

Outside the house were several bundles of rods which my father had been using to make eel-pots. Grandma took one of these rods, made a quick grab for me, and gave me the most terrible whacking. When I finally escaped, I ran to my mother, who was lying in bed, full with child. She took me in her arms and soothed me as best she could. That night she gave birth to her seventh child, a boy, who was stillborn. This tragedy cast a gloom over the entire household. A week or so later Mother resumed her household chores and, from then on, my grandmother was forbidden to enter our home again. She passed away in her 95th year.

Between the ages of six and 16, my school days were few and far between—perhaps a couple of days a week—and my grading ended with the fourth book and, of course, addition and subtraction, but I have had many hard lessons since my school days. I was healthy and strong, but small, weighing only 100 pounds at age 13. In later years I started to grow and at 22 was 6 feet tall and weighed 184 pounds. But I had plenty of inner strength—what it takes to make an iron man who would sail the high seas in wooden ships.

One cold morning in November, the lake beside the little red schoolhouse had risen high from a week's rain. The water was very deep, but with the heavy north wind the lake had started to freeze. We had a slide down the steep bank onto the lake, and on this particular morning the water had frozen enough to bear a man's weight for perhaps 50 feet. Beyond that was thin ice and open water. Most of the school's 20 children had gathered before the morning bell rang to slide out on the ice, the first of the season.

Charlie Hoskins was perhaps six years old, strong and bright for his age. The children had made many slides before I arrived. I was coming along the shore and around the turn, perhaps a quarter of a mile from them, when Charlie made his last slide. A gust of wind caught him and pushed him toward the edge of the thin ice. He sat down, broke through, and disappeared. The children screamed. I saw what had happened and ran for the place he had gone through. I had learned to swim and dive.

Charlie came up, his head out and his hand on the ice, but before I could reach him, he went down again. I reached the hole and, without a thought, I went in. My feet struck his little body. I reached down and pulled him to the surface. With my best efforts I could only shimmy him partly out. His head and breast lay on the thin ice and the quick frost froze his coat sleeve fast in a few seconds. I saw I had no chance. Just when I had about lost hope, Neil McGinnis, who had heard the children's screams from his barn, came running, tearing a pole from the fence as he ran. He shoved it out to me. I had trembling hands and a chilled body but enough strength left to grab the pole. When McGinnis pulled me out, I grabbed Charlie, and they hauled us to the shore. We were both in bad condition.

We had the right man on the job: McGinnis had once been a lifesaver on lonely Sable Island. McGinnis at once carried Charlie into the schoolhouse, where there was a big woodstove full of heat, and laid him on the floor, while one of the bigger boys ran home for a woollen blanket. McGinnis pulled off his jersey, which one of the boys heated while he stripped the clothes from the boy. He wound the hot jersey around Charlie's body, then the hot blanket around that. You could hear Charlie groaning and see him shivering. McGinnis had him back to life again. As for me, I had already made tracks for home—and none too soon: my clothes had to be cut from my body. I had already fallen several times before my mother saw me coming across the fields. She carried me home.

Sometime later Charlie's father, a successful farmer, and his mother, a teacher in the school, came over to our house and talked with my father. They took me in their arms and kissed me. They said they would like to reward me or my family with, perhaps, a cow or a steer, or something for my great courage.

With six small children, we were very poor, but my father refused any reward. The last I heard of Charlie Hoskins, he was a mill man in the Upper Provinces. That was my first real test of courage in life-saving. I agreed to work with Mr. Hoskins on his farm for $2 a week. I helped do the chores around the farm till the end of the year.

The wrecks of the *Etta Stewart* and *Dorcas*

Along the long coastline from Cape Sable to Cape Race, Newfoundland, many have drowned. Sometimes I've wandered to a high cliff or headland and looked out over the great Atlantic. How peaceful and calm at times, with the sun shining down, making the surface so still, so motionless. Sometimes, way off low on the horizon, a white sail is visible and, as you stand there and gaze at it, you wonder what the boat might be doing—perhaps it is a fishing schooner or a coaster. You turn and walk away and probably say to yourself, "I saw this great Atlantic at its best."

Later, perhaps the next week, you walk down again and look out at the sea—but how different it is. What a gale is blowing—the howling wind southeast perhaps 45 or 50 miles per hour—the seas raging, dashing up against the cliffs, and the ocean that was calm and peaceful but a few short days ago now at its worst, a mass of raging breakers.

In my 13th year, I witnessed the face of the Atlantic in perhaps the worst southeast gale and sea that ever smashed over the coastline. The oldest fisherman called it the worst of tragedies that morning when great Atlantic combers, a mass of breakers from the bottom, crashed for miles out to sea.

As I remember it, the *Etta Stewart*, a towboat, and *Dorcas*, a barge, had left Sydney, Cape Breton, the day before, both heavily loaded with coal bound for Halifax. Instead of leaving at 8 a.m., they were delayed, and sailed at 10 a.m. But for the delay and a distance of perhaps 12 miles they would have been out of danger and safe in Halifax harbour before the hauling of the wind to the southwest, for the wind hauled at midnight from southeast to southwest in less than an hour. Nobody could live in those conditions.

We had been fishing at our camp across the harbour the day before the storm; we saw the storm coming up and left for home in the late afternoon. We rowed across the harbour and hauled up our boat at Graham Head near the reef that formed the west side of Three Fathom Harbour. Never before had we hauled our boat up in this dangerous position. From there we walked home, perhaps a distance of 2 miles. The tide was rising very high and the wind increasing; everything indicated a gale. At 3 a.m., the wind struck the cottage from the southwest, which meant that it had jumped from southeast to southwest within a few minutes. With the howl of the wind my father thought of our boat, and called me. Within a few minutes we were on our way back to the reef at Graham Head.

After battling the gusts for 1 mile, we reached the seashore. Though still dark we could see how terrible the gale was. We had only gone a few yards when we came to some wreckage and some rigging which must have washed in the bay before the hauling of the wind. Though the wind blew from the southeast, perhaps 50 miles per hour, it was perhaps 90 miles per hour when it hauled southwest. As we slowly walked the next mile down to the reef, the cold grey dawn began to break in the east, and never in my 60 years of seagoing have I ever seen anything like that morning. As far as the eye could see, the great combers broke from the bottom and rolled again and again till they smashed against the shoreline.

We secured our boat and then stood on the high land to view the angry sea. We had cut a small line, perhaps 6 fathoms long, and had carried it with us. From where we stood, we saw, perhaps 1 mile out, what looked like a large dismasted schooner: she piled high on the crest of a great sea and disappeared for a few minutes, and came to the surface again, bottom-up.

Within the next few minutes the tide and the sea were washing over the reef and in the deep waters of the harbour. But this was not all. At that very time, less than 2 miles west, appeared another wreck raised high on a great wall of water, turned bottom-up and split in two, and the great wooden sides washed ashore along with her crew of 14. As we looked down again on the reef, a large sea was just ready to break, and standing up in it was a man. For a few seconds, it looked as if he were alive, but the next sea caught him up and carried him into the deep waters of the harbour.

Father kicked off his boots and tied the small rope around his waist. He gave me the end to hold. It was his lifeline. We were ready for the next wave, and did not have long to wait. In came a 200-pounder, and Father had but a few seconds. He made a dash, and grabbed the man. Father was very strong and a good swimmer, but the seas knocked him down. He held on to the man, and I dragged in the line.

Father had hauled in five men when we saw what looked like a bunch of seagrass. It was the head of a beautiful young girl, about 16 years old. Her long black hair spread out over her face and shoulders. My father grabbed her arms just as a terrible comber broke against his back, carrying them out into the deep water. I did not see them for perhaps two minutes, but they came to the surface and he still had the girl by the wrist, and his grip was not easily broken. I pulled them in, but he did not let go. To make the load lighter, I spoke to him to let go; I took hold of his hand, and he came to himself and got up just as another woman disappeared over the reef.

We had six on the beach, their bodies still warm and blood running from their bruised bodies—but there were more. The tide was now high and the water deeper on the reef. The job was very dangerous but we pulled in three more. Then the sun rose over that terrible surface, and we waited, but there were no more.

The wind hauled west and moderated. Three men were coming down over the headland. They had seen us. A boat also rowed across the harbour and in the stern of that boat they had a dead man. More help arrived, and we made a large box up on the bank and placed the bodies in it while my father went home and hitched up the horse and drove into town to make a report.

The barge washed ashore 1 mile west, and at daylight the neighbours arrived. The crew had all washed up on the beach. This disaster happened in the days when coal was carried by barge between Halifax and Sydney. The *Dorcas*, a French barge, was a wooden ship dismantled of spars and rigging. That day the barge carried a few passengers and that was the reason for the women being on board. The young girl was said to be going with her chaperone to the city to take her examinations.

The following week, when the news spread, people came from

far and near, and all the teams for miles around drove to Graham Head to view these poor souls and the wrecks of that September gale.

FIRST VOYAGES

I was 14 years old and working for $7 a month on the deck of a 60-ton bluenose schooner. It was as full of bugs as a rat is full of tricks. This schooner lay at Smith's wharf in Halifax harbour loading barrels and general cargo, heading all the way to Goose Bay, Labrador. The first day I put my feet on her deck it had been raining for 12 hours. With me went my empty stomach; the few clothes that I had on were drenched, and I was cold. I had walked some 20 miles from the country to look for anything like work that would keep the spark of life in my young body. For a minute or two I stood on the planks of the wharf and gazed at her black spars and rigging, her main topmast all ready, and I could feel myself climbing up that rigging. But I spoke to myself quietly, "Bill, you are very hungry. You have not had one mouthful of food since early morning."

Having plenty of what it takes to make a man—courage—I jumped down on deck near the first companionway. I got a whiff of pork frying and, sure enough, there was a grey-haired man at the stove. With a voice that sounded like William Tell's, I asked, "Can I come down?" In broken English he kindly answered, "Yes, boy, come down." He thought I was some boy from the shore to see the captain, whom he told me would be back in a few minutes. At once he poured me a cup of hot coffee and let me sample some of his fried pork. I did not have to wait long. A tall, bearded man with a well-seasoned voice sang out, "Come aft, cook, I want to give you some money." The cook was the only other man on board. The cook called out, "There's a boy down here to see you, sir!" "Bring him aft," the captain called back, and off we went. The captain gave the cook $20, which looked like a fortune to me, and told him to take in ship's stores the next morning.

The captain hadn't even looked at me. Then, with a smiling light in his blue eyes, he said, "You are a very wet boy. Have you no raincoat? I had better give you a little drop of rum. It will not hurt you a bit. Then go forward and the cook will give you something to eat. I know you are hungry, and we could use you very well on board." I had not even spoken but, feeling quite satisfied with the kind words, I obeyed orders.

In a few minutes the captain came down to the forecastle and gave the cook orders about the crew coming on board. In the meantime the cook had found out from me that I was the son of a fisherman and wanted to go to sea. As the captain was about to go back on shore again, the cook spoke for me. The deep-sea captain of 70 years looked me over and asked me my name. He also asked if I knew the compass. Without any definite answers, he told me to go aft, keep the fires going, clean the cabin light, and dry my clothes. He would not be back on board till 8 a.m.

I had a dry, warm place to sleep, but that night I was bitten by things that I had never felt before in my young life. I fought with them all through the long night and moved to three different bunks. In the early morning, I put on my dry clothes and hit the deck, my body, hands, and face covered with bites and red blotches. I thought I had contracted measles, or even smallpox, from the cold, or perhaps from the rum he had given me. After I told the cook, he named these things that chased me from bunk to bunk. He got me more contented after telling me they were sea nippers.

At 9 a.m., the captain came up with a bucket and rubber boots and gave me a broom. He drew the water and dashed it on the deck and I, in my bare feet, commenced to scrub with the broom. We threw down all her running gear and re-coiled it on the pins, and all the time the cappy showed me the pins and the right-hand coil. We were perhaps two hours cleaning up the deck and scrubbing her down. The cook called "Come and get it," and we did, but not before we went back in the cabin and had a little nip of rum.

We went down to dinner and his conversation with the cook ran something like this: "I watched this boy work this morning and I am going to fit him out with clothes and shin boots and make a sailor out of him." After dinner we went up to the outfitters store and he not only changed me in clothes but he changed me for life.

The schooner had returned from Newfoundland with a load of herring and took this charter without being cleaned out. On the morning of my third day, down came the crew: the mate, an old-country Frenchman, perhaps 50; a Swede, 25; and a boy of perhaps 16. This was our crew in full. The young fellow became my buddy and first shipmate. We both learned to box the compass and steer.

Under the keen eye of the captain nothing went unseen. We were taught to go up the starboard rigging and come down the port rigging, as the main mast was rattled down. We learned to shift the gaff to, sail, track, and sheet before we ever left the harbour; we learned the time to strike the bells and the time to call the watch. The schooner had three jibs, and we learned the down holes and the pins where the halyards were belayed. We were three days loading cargo, barrels, and supplies for the lobster cannery and a few empty puncheons on deck.

The captain had gone home when we finished the cargo and put the covers on the hatches. We were ready for supper when 20 empty puncheons were hauled down off the wharf; we hoisted them on deck and placed them along the rail. After supper we started to lash them into place. The Swede noticed one had a gallon of black rum in it, which was drawn off. In less than 30 minutes he was drunk, and soon he had many friends drinking with him. The captain had taken me home that evening to bring his wash bag; I had just returned when the cook sent me back to tell the captain to come down. I lost no time in doing so.

Within a few minutes we were on our way back. The Swede and two of his buddies were staggering up the wharf with a bucket half full of rum. I met the bunch on the wharf and the Swede was trying to force me to take rum, saying it was good for me, when the captain came around the corner. He told the Swede to go back on board and get in his bunk. This did not please the Swede, and he wanted to fight, but the captain knew a little trick: he took the bucket of rum and poured it over the Swede's back. The Swede, wet with the rum, smelled worse than the puncheon, and he staggered down on board to change his clothes. He was so drunk that he never got back out of his cabin, and the next morning we got under way while he lay drunk in his bunk.

We had a fresh nor'wester, and the sea was smooth. My feet were no longer on God's green earth. Already I could feel the thrill of the white sail, the squeaking of the blocks, and the list of the deck. The lower sails were all set. "We better set the gaff topsail," the mate said. "This is my first real job of sailor-raising, Bill. Go aloft and loose the topsail." I flew to the weather main rigging and in a minute I was on the crosstrees, lashed her, hooked on the sheet, and threw the tack down on the weather side, went ahead on the halyards, coiled up the gasket, and came down. My first lesson was completed without a mistake.

At 10 a.m., the schooner's prow was pointed eastward. I felt a little homesick, which turned me on my beam end for a while. But we had a great run down the eastern shore. At noon we set the watch and three men put in the watch cleaning up the deck and pumping her out, while we pushed the waves from her bow. My buddy and I had a trick at the wheel and a lesson on course and compass. He was a year older but lacked my quickness.

Along with my new outfit I had a nice new Green River sheath knife and belt for my waist, and this I was very proud of. We had a light cargo with empty puncheons on deck. Down the coast and through the Strait of Canso for the east point of Prince Edward Island we went. About halfway across came out a nor'wester and hit back with a squall. While we were taking in the mainsail, she plunged in forward and snapped off a jib boom that had cut loose under her starboard bow. It looked as if it would smash into my bunk in the forecastle, but eventually we got the main boom crotched and the sail furled and then we took over the jib boom and headsails.

The night was dark and the job mean. Everything was flying loose but the bowsprit. Eventually someone had to go out on the end of the bowsprit to cut the lanyards of the jib-boom foot ropes so we could haul it on board. This is when I tried out my new knife. I went, perhaps 10 feet, and, with my knife in hand and a rope around my waist, I cut a lanyard off, all right. It was not the right one—it belonged to the rope I was standing on—and I disappeared under the bow. That was the last I ever saw of my new knife and pretty near the last they ever saw of me alive, for the rope that was around my waist was caught under the bow and held me from coming to the surface.

I could handle myself as a swimmer, but I had no chance to try. One quick thought saved me: I slipped the rope off my body and came up at the lee rail, while they were still hauling on my lifeline. The captain was at the wheel and did not know anything had happened to me. When I crawled on board in the darkness—there were no lights in those days—he thought we had run down a fishing boat; when I ran forward, they were still trying to clear my lifeline.

By the time we got cleaned up, the stars were shining and the wind was west again. We had a little hot rum and relieved the watch. We made a fairly quick passage, discharged at Goose Bay, and then started picking up a cargo of herring, cod, and lobsters along the coast. While anchored one fine afternoon my buddy and I, both sons of fishermen and well versed in the handling of boats, took the double dory from the deck and rowed up the river with the high tide and loaded her with blocks from the shingle mill. We loaded both ends full. In the middle there was a bucket and some rope. The load in the two ends made her top-heavy. We went down the river all right, but the tide had fallen, leaving a sandbar awash at the mouth. The boat went over this okay and met the heavy sea that was breaking against the tide: we rolled over, bottom-up.

I crawled up on the bottom of the boat. My friend couldn't swim. I looked and I could see the rope trailing, so I dove under: there was my mate head-down and feet-up, under the bottom of the dory. The rope had twined around his neck and was holding him under. I realized his plight and dove under the dory. I had lost my knife but his was looking right at me. I cut the rope that held him and grabbed his long black hair in my hands and pulled him from under the dory, grabbed the plug strap, and, with the other hand, kept him afloat. The captain saw the accident and, with two fishermen who were on deck, with their boat tied astern, came to our rescue. After a few rollers and a punch or two in the middle section, my friend started letting out salt water and, with a little drop of rum, soon came out of it, none the worse.

We made a fairly quick passage home, cleaned up the old bird, and made two more trips to finish up before Christmas. Unfortunately, my shipmate fell off a lobster boat and drowned the next summer.

The *Maud Palmer*

About the first of December I arrived at my cottage home again, a little larger, a little wiser, and with a little money, which I shared with my mother and family. I spent January and February at home and then packed my things in my grandfather's chest. I put it in the back of the wooden sleigh, as the snow and ice were plenty thick on the 24th of February when my mother and I set off.

We arrived at the Halifax side of the harbour about 11 a.m. There, near the ferry wharf, was an acquaintance and lifelong sailor, a black rigger with a wooden leg. The little shack which housed his rigging gear had been his home for many years. I threw my outfit in his shack while my mother bade me goodbye. I got all the news the rigger had collected around the waterfront. He pointed to the spars of a large four-masted schooner flying the Stars and Stripes. She had finished discharging a load of hard coal, so he hobbled along with me to the schooner.

The mate of this schooner was a deep-sea man known as Mr. Allen. We went on board, found him, and went aft to the mate's room. We sat down at a little table, and at once they poured out a little spot of rum. The conversation started with the rigger telling Mr. Allen, "I have already given this boy of mine six months' training. I know his father and mother very well. She left him in my care two hours ago. I want you to find a place for him and let me know every once in a while how he is coming along under fire."

Little more was said. My name and age were taken; the mate asked me where my clothes were and if I wanted to come on board that night. It was all settled in a few minutes, and in no time my few belongings were in my bunk in the *Maud Palmer* starboard forecastle. With four more of the crew I sat down to my first good plateful of Boston baked beans, gingerbread, and cold corned beef—the best I had ever tasted. After supper I was called aft and introduced to the captain, and made a watchman for that night, as the mate was going away till noon the next day. I had confidence in myself, and I carried out my duties to the letter. Twice during the night a policeman came down and got a cup of hot coffee after calling, "Are you there?" I answered, "Yes." I kept the job till I became second mate two years later.

The next day Mr. Allen came back on board, found everything okay, and gave me $10 and the afternoon off. The next morning we signed on part of the crew and pulled out in the stream, anchored, and waited two days for orders. During this time my father rowed alongside in a little boat and asked if they had a young fellow named Crowell on board. The mate called me over to the ship's rail to see if I knew him. I said, "That's my father." The ladder was thrown over and he was welcomed aboard. Father had a parcel of warm socks and mittens for me. At once the mate and Father had an interesting talk of old times, and the mate took him to the cabin for dinner. When my father got ready to go, I gave him $5. The mate said that I had a ship as long as I wanted to stay and that I looked like a promising young man. I bid Father farewell, and I didn't see him again for nearly six years.

We sailed with a nor'wester for Baltimore to load coal for South America. We were about 15 days going over, flying light, and we got caught in a sou'easter and had to anchor off Atlantic City. We rode out that gale in about 17 fathoms of water to anchor, but two other ships did not ride it out and nine members of one crew were lost.

I never will forget that storm—the big schooner rising over those terrible seas and smashing down, and the chain (100 fathoms) out ahead of us. We rode it out and anchored for 24 hours. Then the wind came west, and we sailed again for Baltimore. We loaded 2,600 tons and sailed west to South America and discharged, and loaded timber for Boston, discharged and loaded coal again.

We always had to sign up a new crew. We had two reliable men: the donkeyman, who worked in the ship's engine room, and the cook. The donkeyman was a German engineer and the cook was a Cuban and often acted as an interpreter. We loaded coal, sailed south again, and loaded sugar in sacks for Yonkers, New York, discharged and loaded coal again, this time for Havana, Cuba, discharged and loaded sugar again. This time we signed up a crew of black men to work cargo. Well, when they came aboard I was promoted to second mate, though I was not yet 18. We were loaded and ready for the sea when the eight came on board. When the towboat brought them, I was at my place at the rail. I gave them their orders, told them where to put their clothes, and asked them to come on deck and answer to their names. They gave me the once-over, and one big fellow asked, "Is you the captain's son?" They proved to be good sailors but wanted their own way.

I had four good men in my watch who knew their work, but the mate had two stubborn men—one fellow named Green was a big, strong man of perhaps 30, who had words with the cook, the mate, and the donkeyman. Green would go in the donkey room and take anything he wanted without asking. This did not suit the donkeyman, so he ordered him to keep out. He did not listen. So the next time Green went in, the donkeyman put a .44 against his ribs. He did not go in again. He gave the donkeyman a calling down and said what he could do to him and any white man on board.

I heard this and I did not like it very much. The first chance I got I talked it over with the captain and the mate. I told them I was not afraid of Green and that the next time he made an insulting remark I would order him to shut up. This was a surprise, but they said it was the right thing to do. The captain said he would have the police boat come alongside and have Green locked up as soon as the ship made port, but I said to wait till after I was done with him. One night we called the watch to take in the topsails in my watch and tacked ship, and when we called the mate's watch, we set them on the other tack. Two of my men went up on the fore and main and the mates on the mizzen and spanker. Green came out first. I sent him up to shift tack. The night was fine and calm. He said something when he got up on the sheer poles to go aloft. I heard what he said and the mate was standing near the after-hatch and called out, "What did he say?" I told him I would find out when he came down, but he stayed longer than was necessary, so I went aloft to find out what was keeping him. I saw there was trouble, so I ordered him down at once. He lost no time getting down. When I got down, the mate had called the cook and the donkeyman. He told them we were going to have a little trouble on deck. Green was down first and told the man I was a liar and he was going to lick me or anybody else that interfered. I told him to get ready, just to take off his knife and give it to the mate. I had no weapons and I was going to give him the worst beating he ever had with just my hands. I did not do badly, considering the brute I had to face.

We fought pretty evenly for perhaps 16 minutes, then he knocked me down with a right-hand punch full in the breast. The mate stepped between us till I got up, and I heard him say, "You are hitting him too much in the face. Hit at his wind." I got right up. I think that knock-down saved the day for me; it made Green a little too anxious and, as he rushed at me, I stepped to one side, for I was like lightning on my feet. My right caught him full in the solar plexus and you could hear him grunt all over the deck. He went down on one knee and the mate ordered him up to fight. He staggered to his feet and, when I hit at him again, he grabbed my arm and we went into a clinch. This was allowed in a fight on board ship, but no biting or kicking. He had not quite recovered from my right yet and, after some five minutes, I threw him, but he held me and I landed on top with my left arm on his face and his right arm around my body. It was long and strong and he did not let me up but drove his teeth into the muscle of my left arm; he only could get the skin, but it held me. I reached down and, with my free right hand, I taught him a trick worth two of his. In less than 10 seconds his whole body went limp. I got up. He rolled over face-down and grunted. The mate told two of his watch to help him to his bunk. I went aft to the cabin and had my hand treated. Our blood was all over everybody, and the deck had to be washed up. I still wear his teeth marks.

The captain and mate were well satisfied with the night's work and told me I had a berth on the schooner as long as there was one. At four bells my watch was out again. The mate called me and asked me if I could make it. In five minutes I was on deck, with black eyes and in poor condition. I stayed on deck for my two-hour watch. Eight bells called the mate's watch again, but Green would not get up, so the mate went to his bunk and made him get out. He climbed out and I waited till he came on deck, and I shook hands with him.

We finished out the voyage, discharged, and I took my much-treasured sea chest and signed off. I met my first shore buddy as he was packing his bag from a little schooner at the same pier—a young Swede, perhaps 20. He could speak English and was well acquainted with the hangouts. We roomed together at a boarding house in Brooklyn, New York, and became good friends.

After one month of real fast going, we picked up a four-masted ship loading oil in cases for the Dutch East Indies, the *Curzon*.

Three years on the *Curzon*

The *Curzon* was a square-rigged ship that carried case oil for Astral Oil Works. Specializing in illuminating oil, which had previously been derived from whale oil, the products of the Astral Oil Works kerosene refinery became famous in the late 19th century, giving rise to the slogan, "The holy lamps of Tibet are primed with Astral Oil."

The *Curzon* was loaded with case oil bound for the Dutch East Indies, carrying a crew of 32, officers and all: Captain Black, a Welshman of perhaps 65, as well as three mates, a boatswain, sailmakers, carpenters, a donkeyman, a cabin boy, two ordinary seamen, four apprentices, and a cook from South Africa, known as a Boer.

On board, the second mate did the talking. When we all lined up, he called out our names, and we answered. As the mate called, the first mate picked out the most likely seamen for each watch. Then we went to our quarters. This ship's forecastle was under the foredeck and in the centre of this stood the ship's windlass and all its equipment. Bunks were on each side in two rows, perhaps 20 narrow boxes in which each man placed his mattress and blanket. These were to be his quarters for three years.

What a mean place. We ate our food on the floor, washed from a bucket when we could catch the water, and had the poorest and meanest food that could be rationed for a ship. Our crew consisted of 12 Americans, two Germans, a Bluenose (me), four Norwegians, and three Swedes.

We were called back to the after-hatch and had the articles read to us by the captain and the usual orders, "Yes, sir," "No, sir," to the officers. When eight bells rang, we went to the galley for our first meal, which consisted of a not-too-well-done stew. It was dished out to us in our pans and served with one slice of bread and a mug of black coffee. We had one hour for a smoke and then we cleaned up the deck, pumped out the ship, coiled down the running gear, and got ready to get under way in the early morning. During the afternoon I made friends with one of the Germans, a young man apparently not a sailor but a good swimmer.

The July night was fine and a little wind blew from the southwest. My buddy and I slept on deck covered with our blankets. A three-masted schooner lay perhaps 50 yards from us. The third mate was watchman during the night, but nevertheless this fellow went over the bow and down the chain and swam perhaps 25 yards before the watchman saw him. He went aft and called the first mate, who came up with a pistol and called the German to come back, but he was well out of reach. Still, the mate fired two shots in his direction.

This delayed our sailing till noon the next day when the captain came on board with a little cockney seaman. The cocky little fellow was a good square-rig sailor, but he was a troublemaker. The captain did not have his feet on deck before he gave orders to get under way, so nine men went aloft to loosen her down, while the rest of the crew started to heave her short. The four apprentices tended the men aloft from the deck buntlines and halyards and whatever they wanted done. At dark that night the towboat let us go off Sandy Hook. We blew a farewell blast and bade goodbye to the Statue of Liberty. Many of the crew would never see it again.

During the last week on shore I lost my appetite and had pains in my head. I did not know it then, but in the next month I was going to hang at death's door with malarial fever. At the end of my watch that night I turned in, and remained there for 22 days. The next morning, when called, I fell from my bunk to the floor. My buddy from the other side of the forecastle was by my side in a minute. They picked me up, put me back in my bunk, and called the captain, who came and took my temperature. He found that I was raging with malaria and at once put a watch at my bunk while he prepared salts and quinine—an old ship remedy. He declared it too late for my recovery. I cannot explain my condition for the next few days as I laid there out of my mind and calling "Mother" whenever I came to. The captain kept me asleep as much as possible. He knew what to do and what to give me. He stayed with me many hours. One morning I opened my eyes and groaned. I was awake and living. The quinine had done its work. He gave me a couple of spoonfuls of water and cooled my forehead as best he could, and I was on the road to recovery.

Blow the man down,
Blow him right down
Give me some time to blow the man down.

As we slowly sailed over that long trail toward the Cape of Good Hope, at the southern end of South Africa, we enjoyed fine weather and plenty of sunshine. It made the passage down to the Cape, a rocky headland known for stormy weather and rough seas, long but life-saving for me. After some 25 days I again learned to walk and move around the deck, and then to steer. As my strength began to return, I put in many long hours at the wheel and learned to make and repair sails. For two months I did not leave the deck, although we had a lot of handling sails and working ship. We wore our old sails and were not prepared for any heavier weather.

We were getting well along on our first leg when we picked up a bad squall that seemed to come from nowhere in particular. Within 30 minutes it left us under bare poles, except for our lower courses. They were good sails and worn as standbys, but they kept us sailing. The rest of our 25 upper sails left the yards in ribbons. In all my five years of square-rigging, I had never seen a ship stripped of her glad rags in 30 minutes, before anything could be done. We cleared and hung our three lower topsails first. This made the ship manageable. All hands were on deck for eight hours, till 6 p.m., when the port watch went below for two hours. At eight bells the starboard watch took over. The night was dark, the wind fresh and fair, and she quietly sailed through the night. At 6 a.m., all hands worked on deck till we got her in full dress again. During this procedure I steered 14 hours and had but one glass of brandy and a bowl of soup. I left the wheel very tired.

The rest of the run down to the Cape we enjoyed fine weather and fair wind. Every day I gained in health and strength. I grew 2 inches in height and went up to 190 pounds. Though I received a lot of abuse from the crew aboard about not being able to do my work, I went slowly and learned the many things that had to be done by an able-bodied seaman. After I was able to go aloft, and take my own part, I did not fear the orders which would have been impossible for me to handle at the beginning of the voyage. Captain Black and his second mate kept me on the road to recovery. Along with my buddy they carried an extra load for me many times.

Near the Cape

We had a few fine days around the Cape; one morning as I went aft to relieve the wheel, I saw my first albatross, a large bird found near the Cape of Good Hope. It weighs between 15 and 40 pounds and is maybe 7 feet from wing tip to wing tip. They fly perhaps 12 strokes of the wing, and then glide. There is quite a history to these birds, which many square-rig seamen delight in telling. Captains and officers would not allow these birds to be caught, or killed. It was considered bad luck to kill or capture one of these magnificent birds. Our little cockney told us that all captains and officers lost rounding the Cape come back, or at least their souls return, in these birds.

The birds follow the ships for hours, feeding on whatever is thrown overboard. They came close to the ship, but I never remember seeing them settle on its surface. Many sailors caught these birds in the early morning while the captain slept, if the officer in charge allowed it. They took a piece of thin metal, cut it in a "V," wired a small piece of meat in the centre and towed it astern, perhaps 50 feet behind the boat. When the bird dove down to pick it up, its heavy bill, which is larger at the end, got caught in the V, and it was trapped.

On the poop deck, one morning at daybreak, the cockney and the second and third mates were there with a line and bait while the watch stood near the cabin door. Two lines were out, one with a V and the other with a sail hook and bait. We did not have long to wait as they both hooked birds within a few minutes. The cockney was going to stuff these birds. He wanted four. It did not take long, as they sailed right on board and, when they landed on deck, one blow from the pin killed them. In less than 30 minutes he had them in the chain locker, and over the next three months he stuffed and mounted them. Their bodies were filled with oakum, a preparation of tarred fibre used for caulking or packing the joints of timbers in wooden ships. In his sea chest the cockney had everything to do this work; when he finished, it was a credit to any professional.

After a three-day run we noticed a small tramp steamer hauling out on our course. On the morning of the third day, the wind moderated and, at noon, she was astern and very close. Late in the evening she was aft the beam and within hailing distance. She ran up a small pennant flag, and we could see from the bridge that a man was going to give us a message. All hands came on deck and lined the rail to listen. From his megaphone, he yelled, "President McKinley has been assassinated." The president was shot, and fatally wounded, on September 6, 1901, on the grounds of the Pan-American Exposition in Buffalo, New York. He died several days later.

We hoisted our answer pennant, and he hauled his down. The conversation was over. His was the only voice we heard outside of the ship's company for six months. After four months we anchored in the Strait of Batavia, where we became becalmed and started to drift in under a burning volcano. We sounded and found we had 80 fathoms of water, but we anchored and set a double anchor watch to keep the local people away. They came in dugouts, rafts, and all manner of rudely constructed boats, from where I never did know, with beasts, birds, shells, eggs, and monkeys. Many lined the deck. The officer gave one hour's permission before dark. They were coming from all directions and climbing on board and, as they did not want to leave when asked to do so, the captain ordered "All hands on deck."

The officers got their firearms and fired over their heads. I never saw human beings disappear so quickly in all my seagoing days. With the crack of a 12-gauge shotgun they jumped or fell overboard and started to swim to their boats or for the shore, leaving many of their belongings behind. I feared for the lives of some of them. After all was clear the captain called two boats alongside and gave them their belongings. We traded with them a little the next day. We had to stay there for five days till we got a fair wind. We had to cover our lights and cabin skylight and everything that was easily broken as torrents of heat and lava belched out of the volcano. Great pieces of pumice stone hit the deck and the water for miles around. Never shall I forget those five days. We put sails up over the forward and after decks to keep the sun from burning us and kept the hand pump and hose going morning and night for the ship's hold was filled with case oil.

In the early morning of the sixth day, a leading wind sprang up and everything indicated a breeze. We started the iron mick (the capstan, a vertical-axle rotating machine to apply force to ropes and cables) with six long bars and three men on each bar and around and around she went till the anchor was up. Everyone was anxious to get clear of this hellish place, so the slack chain came in pretty fast, about 200 feet per hour. The shanty singer was our third mate, and for six hours we had 30 men on these bars and we sang every shanty that was ever sung before that anchor came to the surface. At last it hung on the cathead, and what a tired and worn-out crew we were, covered with dust, and with a path around the windlass 6 inches deep in lava and stones from the volcano. Several men had lumps on their heads from the flying stones. My buddy was a man of great vitality, perhaps one of the best on board, and many times he asked me if I felt the effects of this grind. It did wear on the calves of my legs, but after a few days I was perhaps the hardiest man on board.

The wind carried us through the strait and out into the bay, when we sighted a small barque with its distress signals up. Though we still had about 70 miles to get to the coast, we drifted in the bay for many hours. The barque was from Italy and had sailed 14 days ahead of us, loaded with oil and a crew of 12. She had made somewhat of a longer passage as she did not come through the strait, but in the last 300 miles had struck headwinds and heavy rain, while we had mostly fair winds and burning sun. We towed her in shoal water, 3 miles from the coast. Her distress signals were sincere. Out of the 12 men on board she had five dead on the main hatch, covered over, and only four men able to walk. There was a large hospital up on the mountain where we took them.

We lay 3 miles from the harbour and unloaded in small lighters from 1,000 to 5,000 cases a load. We were more of a warehouse than a cargo ship. The captain went to the mountain hospital and the first mate was left in charge. Seven months had passed from the time we left New York.

We had a steam donkey, a common name for a steam-powered winch or logging engine that was fired with coal and stood on deck near the after-hatch. It was used for hoisting cargo, eight cases in a sling. On the port side of the ship a stage was built up with one end on the ship's rail; under this stage was about three tons of dry sand so that if a man fell off he would not get hurt. Here the hatch tender stood with a whistle attached to a cord around his neck. He blew "hoist lower." We had an awning over the stage, as it was very hot.

The water was bad here and we did not have much fresh food. I remember that potatoes cost $9 a bushel. We had one bushel for our Christmas dinner. We had as much gin and quinine melted in water as we wanted to drink to prevent dreaded diseases.

We had been working a few days in the heat when, just before dinner, the hatch tender took a severe pain in his head and stomach and fell before he could get down from the stage. We helped him to a place in the shade and another man took the whistle from his neck and finished out the day's work while we ran up the flag for the boarding officer. The doctor looked him over and sent him to shore; we never saw him again. Within the next week three men came down from that stage and, for the last one, two doctors came on board to investigate. They discovered that the germs on the whistle had been spreading the disease. The doctor ordered more fresh food and the fumigation of our quarters. We had been so long on rationed food and poor drinking water that the crew began to quarrel.

Christmas was drawing close and half of our crew members were on shore sick, and four had died. Two days before Christmas our supplies came on board with a few extra things for dinner. In this no man's land there was not much to choose from, but there were 25 live chickens—one for each man—and the Boer cook commenced to prepare dinner.

A big pot of water was placed on the galley stove; each chicken had a string tied around its neck and was stuffed into the pot with the string hanging over the side. When the little cockney passed by the galley door and saw the cook putting the last one in, he asked, "Are you cooking them feathers and all"? He answered, "Yes, that's good enough for you." The cockney said, "Not for me."

Before the cook could reach for his knife, the cockney grabbed the pot and threw it on deck, chickens and all. This brought everybody on deck and although the cook was the only one armed, he did not have a chance. We had a tall Finn who took over the galley for one day with orders from the chief mate to prepare dinner for the crew and whatever food there was for our dinner. When the chickens, and the fight, cooled off, we each picked up our bird, cleaned it, and the Finn did the rest.

January passed. We finished discharging and then we loaded ballast with sand from the bottom of the bay. Everything was ready for the captain's return on board with whatever crew I could sign from the shore. When the mate called us aft, there were only 17 of the crew; two of them had returned from the hospital. He told us that, starting at 8 a.m., we could have 24 hours liberty. He gave us 25 guilders and told us not to get drunk or to fight as we would be locked up on sight. The boat would pick up the crew at the end of the 24 hours.

Onshore, myself, a sailmaker, my buddy, and the cabin boy hired a team of donkeys and drove back into the country, perhaps 10 miles. We had lots to eat and drink. The locals who drove us knew the road and many places to go. The next day at 4 p.m. we returned to our boat, well satisfied with our liberty. We danced and sang.

When Jack he goes ashore,
With his gold and silver star
There is no one can get rid of it so soon
For the first thing Jack demands
Is a fiddle at his hand
Choice liquor and cigar of every kind
A pretty girl likewise,
With two dark and rolling eyes,
Then Jack is suited to his mind.

A day later, the last day of January, we left, bound for New-castle, Australia, sailing short five crew members, although we picked up two—a tall Russian Finn and a young German—at Batavia, capital of the Dutch East Indies. Expecting to be at sea for 100 days, we made the passage in 94, but much happened in those three months. As we did not add much to our rations, and our water supply was poor, most of the crew was feeling the effects, and a terrible sickness passed through the ship's company. As for myself, I gained weight. I weighed 194 pounds. Our bread supply was poor hard tack that had been stored in a big iron tank for perhaps 10 years. When the bread box was brought in, it was infested with maggots. Each biscuit had to be knocked on something several times to dispose of the insects.

I was terribly fed up with what I had already experienced on the ship and planned to get out from under the British flag as soon as we reached New South Wales. I did not like this English ship—$14 per month, and rationed food. Everything but murder had taken place on the ship. I had long made up my mind that an American ship would carry me from Australia, but the captain and the mate thought differently. I had to buy my discharge for one month's pay. I ended up staying in Australia for six weeks before setting sail again.

Over 100 sails lay in Newcastle harbour. One was a full-rigged ship tied at the coal pier, waiting orders to load coal for Dewey's fleet at Manila. She was one of the Saints (there were several) in Saint David. There were wooden ships carrying a crew of 17 and paying $25 per month, so my buddy and I went on board, and found we had a berth. We signed on to the American ship and here, as boatswain on the *Saint David*, is where I was left handicapped for the rest of my days on earth.

The *Saint David*

We packed up and changed ships and spent the next 30 days at the dock. As we were the only two able-bodied seamen on board, we began to clean her up and do some rigging under the captain's orders. He was from Maine and had his wife and daughter on board. His wife had been sailing with him for several years, and I learned on our next voyage that she was a fine woman. I had about $80. I sent four $10 gold pieces home to my mother. I never forgot that she needed my help. My buddy started spending his money, and before our 30 days were up he was broke.

On the *Saint David*, we had good clean quarters and good food. We loaded coal for Manila for Dewey's Transport Service. When the loading was finished, we anchored out in the bay, fitted out for the voyage, and signed on a crew of 14—all able seamen and two boys from the town (first voyagers). She was a ship full of coal and very deep in the water, old and run down, but our passage down was perhaps one of the finest in the seven seas. We were lucky to have moderate weather.

The *Saint David* was a three-masted, full-rigged ship, and every day some piece of gear got carried away, so I had to keep the crew working every minute. She had a well-stocked lazarette, a storeroom aft under the wheelhouse where the ship's stores, rope, oakum, and rigging were kept. The first mate was a Norwegian; the second mate, a Bluenoser. The cook was black. We had good food, and plenty of it, and one of the finest crew of men I have ever sailed with. The ship's carpenter was also from Maine and ran the hoist. I looked after the repair of the sails as we had no sailmaker.

The ship was a little too heavy for the small crew she carried. We had light winds and fair weather down the Australian coast, past New Guinea, across the Caroline Islands before we hauled up for Luzon, the largest island in the Philippines. We were somewhere in the Coral Sea with every sail drawing when the man at the wheel saw smoke coming out of the lazarette hatch. I was training two boys, who smoked cigarettes, on board. I kept them busy 12 hours out of 24. I had cleared part of the floor of the lazarette and had them plaiting rovers out of good rope yarns, each perhaps 3 feet long. I tried to stop the boys from smoking cigarettes at work, but while down below they must have been taking a puff. When eight bells struck, they must have thrown down their cigarette butt, and the draft from the hatch blew it under a bale of oakum. Meanwhile, the boys came up, closed the hatch, had dinner, and remained on deck.

Seeing smoke, the mate opened the lazarette hatch. A gush of smoke in the face greeted him. He closed the hatch and rang the fire warning for all hands on deck. We had a force pump that operated with manpower handles. A barrel was placed near the hatch and filled with water by draw buckets with a hose from the barrel to the pump and from the pump to the fire. In about two minutes I had all this in order. I had not looked down the hatch as I had to take my orders from the officer on deck. The mate had given orders to cut a hole in the deck, near the fire, and to shove the hose through. The captain had ordered the course changed and called his wife and daughter on deck. To me things did not look serious.

I lifted the hatch a little. Smoke blew out along with the smell of burning oakum. I could see a small flame in a bale of oakum that had just started to burn its way through the floor. In a flash I decided what to do. My buddy was forward fitting out the ship's boats for the captain; the second mate was trimming the sails, and the first was working aft. The captain was trying to pacify his wife and child. I told the mate what I had in mind and to be ready to lift the hatch. I slipped into a suit of rubber clothes and jumped into the barrel of salt water, sou'wester and all.

I went down the hatch. With my bare hands I grabbed that bale of oakum and threw it up on deck while the flames went up my wet arms and hands. This did not take more than a minute. My hands did not burn very much, but my arms blistered as they got the flames. Next, we directed the hose on the fire and, within a few minutes, had the fire under control.

They got the ship back on course while I got my hand and

arms bandaged up in oil. They were sore for a long time. While I was being treated, the captain decided he was going to see that I was rewarded for my brave action. He felt that I had saved the ship from sinking at sea and perhaps all hands on board. We had a can of black powder, oil, paint, and many flammables on board and, given 10 minutes more, the stern would have blown off. The captain had three barrels of stout on this run for himself. He gave orders to hoist one up on deck; and he gave every man one bottle, which we all enjoyed.

As to my reward, I did not deserve it any more than the rest of the crew, but that is not the law of America. The ship's logbook was brought out at the salon table and as near as I can remember this is what the captain wrote: "In the year nineteen hundred and one, on June third, from Newcastle, N.S.W., in the *Saint David* on passage to Manila, heavily laden with coal, fire was discovered in the lazarette. Day fine, wind S.W., ship running aft, Seaman William Arthur Crowell, born at Dartmouth, Nova Scotia, 20 years of age and boatswain of this ship, did with his bare hands and wet clothes go down in the lazarette and throw a flaming bale of oakum on deck, while smoke and flames poured from the hatchway.

"As a reward for his thought and quickness of performing this almost impossible act, I ask the compassion and awareness of this ship to reward this brave seaman with at least three years of navigation where the same is taught for the purpose of becoming an officer in this line, or any other he feels like sailing on, and this shall be given to him free of charge, or any other reward the owners or any other authority feel should be given to him. Signed Captain John Harrington, and witnessed day of our Lord, nineteen hundred and one, the third day of May."

Well, after that, things happened and neither the captain nor I reached the home port of the ship.

We had a fine run with light wind, and I nursed my sore hands. We were drawing well down toward Luzon when we got becalmed for a couple of days. The sun was pouring down from the heavens, then came a puff of wind from the northeast and the sky clouded. We started to take in our light sails but, before we could get everything in trim, the gale was howling through our rigging. This proved to be the worst gale I had ever lived through. We got her shortened down about dark and the watch went below.

At eight bells, midnight, we called the watch with orders to stand by. We worked for many hours. She had a high poop deck and we ran lifelines along the weather side from forward to the poop as the list of the deck was too great for us to stand up on it. At the height of the wind and sea that commenced to break over her weather bow, it swept every moveable object clear of its lashing, smashed it, or swept it into the sea. The boats on the midship house were blown clear of their lashings, and our sails, many of which had had a second lashing, blew in pieces from the yards.

All overhead sails blew and were washed clear of the jib boom. The sea broke over the forecastle deck and hit the forward part of the ship and struck the midship house and smashed its way through the galley and the carpenter shop. The only place that was left was the donkey room. As the wind began to haul and head the ship aft, the sea broke on our beam ends and we began to drift too closely to the islands.

A long night this was, but at last the cold grey dawn began to break. What a dreary wreck we found. We tried to save some of our sails, but it was not safe to be anywhere on deck or aloft, so we gave up and made shelter in the donkey room. The wheel had relieving tackles, which probably saved our rudder. As daylight broke, the captain thought she might lay better on the other tack, so a large fellow named O'Brien, the second mate named McDonald, and myself worked our way aft and back to the wheelhouse and relieved the wheel from her tackles, hove her down, and waited. She slowly paid off a few points, just enough to bring the sea aft the beam and would not come around. The seas began to board her on the after quarters. One very heavy sea boarded her over the after-weather quarter, smashed in the side of the wheelhouse in which we were standing, swept the after cabin, and smashed the skylight in. The cabin commenced to fill. The captain's wife and child started screaming, believing that the ship was sinking.

Things looked bad. The sails were gone, the cabin skylight smashed, a heavy list to starboard, and heavy seas breaking over her from every angle. To save our lives the skylight had to be covered. In the mizzen rigging was a canvas jack, perhaps 6 by 8 feet, placed against the rigging from the outside, and a small piece of sail that helps to keep the ship's head to wind. We came out of the wheelhouse with ropes tied around our waists and tied fast to the bits, or rings, in the sail. In that wind and sea we cut away the sail and I got up on the cabin and spread the sail over the broken lights. They passed me a hammer, nails, and some boards. At last I got it nailed down. I was just about finished when a sea broke over her quarter and swept me over the side. The end of the heavy gasket or rope that was around me caught and twined around my leg and pulled my left hip out of place. My body was left hanging over the side of the cabin house. They pulled me back on board and carried me in the cabin. After a while I realized my condition. I would be handicapped for the rest of my life.

After battling the gale for 12 hours, finally the wind hauled west and we got the ship around and back on course. I was in bad shape. How I lived for the next 15 days was a miracle. They fitted up a bunk for me in the sail room by hanging a block overhead and making a canvas sling in which they hung my bandaged leg. A rope led from the block to the side of my bunk so that I could hoist or lower it; but every time I moved, I felt pain. Before we got to port, my leg was swollen and turning a deep purple.

It was perhaps three days before they got the ship in sailing order. The wind remained light, and the sun burned everything on deck. My buddy was with me every minute that he could spare from his watch, and the captain's wife was kind to me. There was little they could do for my damaged hip. I just lay there, and suffered. At last we hauled into Manila, but they signalled us not to enter the port. The mate signalled back, "Crew member badly hurt," so they sent a small steam launch out from one of the ships in the bay. I was lowered on board from a stretcher attached to the yardarm. I was carried ashore and an ambulance drove me to the hospital, where I spent the next 96 days.

I had three operations. The head surgeon, Dr. Donnelly, was an Englishman who had come during the Spanish-American War, along with a few American doctors. They did not think I had a chance, as I was only a step ahead of death. But I knew I was strong and full of good rich blood. They did their best, and I got better. I was supposed to be sent home, but the ship remained in Manila for four months. By that time I was walking on crutches. Captain Harrington got sick, and left the ship at Manila. He returned home to Maine. A Captain Rider came out to take her home for repairs, so I went back on board again as a sailmaker and we picked up a crew of beachcombers.

Late in September we left the port of Manila in ballast, bound across the North Pacific—a long passage usually filled with blustery weather. We were fitted out for perhaps two months' passage. We were on our course for perhaps a week with very light winds. Several of the crew had been in the Army and others had just arrived and were glad to get away from Manila. At the end of the first week we had three cases of malaria and dysentery. It was calm for 10 days and the sun was very hot.

We had some repairs done to make the ship seaworthy. During this calm spell one of the crew died; I saw my first burial at sea. Two more would have died only for a bit of good fortune. We were perhaps one month out and already feeling the effects of sun and disease when we saw a large white steamer over the horizon; it proved to be the American *Maru*. We ran up the assistance flag and they lowered a boat and took two of our sick crew and put them in their sick bay. They returned with a boatload of supplies, including a side of fresh beef and a small keg of rum. One of the ship's officers opened a couple of bottles and gave us all a drink.

He also left some medicine. For a few days we all had a new spirit.

We were down past the coast of Japan and got plenty of wind. On the 34th day out we got several squalls from all directions. So quickly did the wind haul around the compass that we could not trim the sails fast enough; she caught a tack and dismasted over the starboard quarters, much of her yards and gear falling on deck. Within the next hour a raging gale from the northeast began to blow and it took us 12 hours till we got cleared of her spars and rigging, saving only a couple of topsail yards to rig for foremasts. Many of her spars pounded against the side and we were afraid they might punch her planks through. At daylight we had her cleared off.

The captain decided he would try to run back to Japan. We rigged up jury masts and hoisted a storm trysail. After a day or so of weather we were again heading for land. We did sight the lights on the coast one night, but, before morning, the wind had jumped from the northeast and blown off the coast again. I remember that late on our next fine Sunday morning we had a little cold weather and placed a large Beehive stove up in the new sail room to make comfortable quarters for the crew.

We had hopes every day of sighting some ship that might tow us to port. We had many sick on board. The sun rose, and the day was clear and cold. The wind was fair, running us along toward the coast of Japan, perhaps 4 miles per hour, when the watch reported, "Boat dead ahead, sir." With the glasses we could see a boat, but with only one man. As we slowly sailed toward her, it proved to be a sampan, a relatively flat-bottomed boat used by the Japanese in harbours. It had blown out to sea eight days before and had drifted, with seven men on board. They use no sail but just scull along with long sweeps, or oars. There had been seven strong men in the boat when they were out in this gale. When we picked them up, by steering dead straight down on them, we found that one was dead. The others were alive, but frozen. Only one could speak.

We made a line, weighted it down in the bow, and pulled up alongside the boat. As we slowly sailed along, we dropped a man down in her with a rope, and hauled five of them on deck. We had prepared new quarters for them. We carried them in, and saved their lives. We had them for the remainder of our voyage and shared our rations with them. Their feet and hands were swollen and broken, as they were frozen clean to the bone. Since I was unable to go aloft, and could still not do very much, I became their nurse. I can hear and see those poor souls suffering to this day.

At the end of 62 days we were picked up by the steamer *Glen Oickle* and towed into Yokohama, Japan. We left the ship there. My square-rigging days were over.

> *It is not the gale, it's the set of the sail*
> *That tells which way she goes.*

Going into steam

I stayed in Yokohama as watchman till they started to repair and get the spars and yards ready. I spent Christmas Day with the Salvation Army, the greatest Christian organization in the world. As the days rolled by, my leg became stronger and I began to walk without my stick. I started to feel like myself once more. I had much time to myself and moved around the docks whenever there was a ship or visited the poor souls in the hospital. They had their arms and legs taken off, but they still lived, and they knew me as their nurse.

After a few more days I began to look for a ship, this time something with power, if possible. One morning in came a new 6,000-ton steamer built in Baltimore, Maryland, for the Maru line. Her American port was Seattle and she was signing on American officers.

A Salvation Army master and myself went on board. I got a berth as boatswain, with a week to look around the ship before we sailed. She carried 20 boys, and I trained them in seamanship. It was good that one of them spoke English. I made three voyages across the Pacific in this ship. It had new, clean rooms and good food.

On our return to Japan on the third voyage we started to discharge cargo late in the afternoon, when an earthquake struck, killing some 20,000 people and causing $1 million in damage. Four of the boys and myself had just landed on the breakwater in a small boat from our ship. I had been teaching them how to row and handle a boat and was standing on the planking when I heard a rumbling sound, from where I could not tell. The boys called "quakie, quakie" and dropped down on their stomachs on the wharf. Within a second, the breakwater went out from under me and I fell on my back. For a few minutes I did not know if I could get up. I felt the shock pretty badly, and right then I decided this would be my last voyage to Japan.

When we returned to Seattle, I signed off and put in the next two years salmon fishing out of Seattle. While there, I swam from a companion towboat to a fish scow, a flat-bottomed boat that had broken adrift and went ashore with a line around my shoulders. I swam 50 yards through a sou'wester and cut a line that held her on a reef. I probably saved the lives of two men and, as the towboat lay head to the sea, they started to pull me back on board, but with so much line out I had a hard battle getting back on board again. I found that I was quite a seal in the water, and for this I received quite a pat on the back.

At the end of the second year I went back to New York and from there home to see my folks. After getting my first mate's ticket for steam and passenger service, I packed my seagoing belongings and booked my next ship.

After 30 days with my family, I went to Halifax and walked around the docks looking for a berth to any part of the world. I was still a little lame, but the short rest at home had done me good. At the pier in the North End lay a three-masted schooner loading plaster rock for the New York Plaster Works. I stepped on board and found a watchman on deck. He told me they were loading rock for New York and would be signing on a crew as they would be finished the next day. I walked up the dock and met the captain and introduced myself and signed on for the run to New York. We would sail three days later, with a crew of eight men, myself as first mate.

I looked over the ship, read the articles, and then the crew came on board. I had her pumped out and washed off and made ready. On the morning of the third day we hoisted the glad rags. With a fresh nor'wester, we lost sight of Nova Scotia within a few hours. We had made some 300 miles when we found her leaking badly, and for the rest of the passage we were kept busy at the pumps. We were 13 days to Sandy Hook, along the coast of eastern New Jersey. We picked up a light breeze south and ran up to Hell Gate, New York, and anchored.

On account of the tide we laid very close to the wreckage of a paddle-wheel excursion ship, *Benjamin Slocumb*, that had caught fire while on a cruise with 2,000 teachers and schoolchildren on board. While coming up from Sandy Hook, the story goes, she caught on fire forward. While the flames swept over her deck, the captain kept her going full speed. Teachers and children crowded aft to get clear of the flames, which burned the wooden accommodations on deck. Hundreds of them fell overboard, screaming with fear. All this could have been avoided had he stopped and turned her stern to the wind. After some miles of this terrible misfortune, he ran her on the ledges at Hell Gate. We anchored close by, and there we saw the charred remains. Hundreds are said to have died in the fire. I think they declared the captain out of his mind. He is said to have served time in an institution where his hair turned snow-white within a few months.

We finished the passage and hauled into the plaster works. I signed off and went to the Big Apple. The next morning I signed on as second mate with the Panama Pacific Steamship Company's Steamship *Alliemae*, which was running from New York to Ceylon (now Sri Lanka) and Central America. It carried freight and passengers to a short railroad that ran from the Atlantic to the

Pacific before the Panama Canal was finished. I held this berth for perhaps six months. In the early spring I went to Boston and Gloucester, Massachusetts.

Fishing out of Gloucester

After spending some time with my mother's people in Boston I got short of money, so I wandered down to the wharf and looked over the fishing fleet. My father was a fisherman and boat builder, and my first money was earned by fishing. I felt the urge to be on a fishing boat again. At the wharf was a little round bow schooner which needed a few hands. I decided to try. I hunted up a dory mate, and we went on board. For dinner we had beef stew and a table full of good food. I thought I would only make one trip, but I found myself there four years later, still fishing.

We fresh-fished in the South Channel, with a crew of 20 young men. Every night in we had a dance at a neighbour's house, or where some of our crew boarded. We were joined by many women and this was the first time I really stepped out. After two months, we sailed for Gloucester and there we tied up for a week of dances, songs, women, and wine. I met a lovely widow, so I packed my bag and hung around for a while. She had a boarding house with 20 rooms and served meals. Lights were out at 2 a.m. In those days we had mostly square dances, waltzes, and polkas. I spent two months ashore during the winter.

Sailing the Grand Banks

I made many trips to the Grand Banks of Newfoundland. A fleet of boats and an army of men fished winter and summer, supplying markets all over the world. Trawling for cod and halibut occurred in the fall or winter seasons. Halibutting requires large hooks rigged 9 feet apart and used in deeper water. Halibut are strong and must be killed before you haul them in the dory. The fish is hit on the end of the back fin that ends near the head and one light tap with an iron gaff kills the fish. It is then hauled in.

On the voyage, we sailed from Gloucester early in February in a 90-ton schooner fitted for the business, ballast floored down, and her hold penned off in blocks to hold perhaps 2,000 pounds of iced fish. Leaving Gloucester we carried bait, probably frozen herring, or fresh if possible. Iced down, they will remain fresh for perhaps three weeks. About 20 barrels and 30 tons of ice were stored in the pens, with boards that fitted across the front of the pens, where we kept food supplies for about four weeks. We carried perhaps eight two-man dories, 17 fishermen, the captain, cook, and sometimes a spare hand.

On this voyage we sailed to Liverpool, Nova Scotia, and took in our ice and bait and sailed for Quero Bank, 30 miles east of Sable Island. We anchored in 55 fathoms of water about February 10, baited our lines, and made a set, as it is called. We found we were on a spot of fish. It was bitter, cold, and rough.

Late in the afternoon of the second day at anchor came signs of a storm. By early the next morning it was getting worse, so we cleared the deck, lashed the dories to the hatch, reefed the riding sail, and paid out cable to make her ride easier. Late the next day the wind went east, and later northeast, making the sea very bad. It turned bitter cold the morning of the third day. The sea was very heavy. The mate and I kept watch over things, including the cable, to see that it did not chafe off at the hawsepipe.

At about 3 p.m., I came on deck to look after the top dories that were freezing up, and about 3 miles to windward I saw a heavy sea breaking. It was perhaps a mile long on the crest and broke heavily, disappearing in white foam. I started to work again, but after a few minutes I felt a lee and looked up to see a great wall of water, perhaps 100 feet tall, dead ahead of the bow of the schooner. She had forged ahead and slacked the cable, just as this monster was coming. I jumped out of the stern of the stack of dories and landed on the jaws of the main gaff and secured a good hold on the tack.

This sea was 3 miles long and 30 feet high and was at its height when it boarded the schooner. It swung her off till the cable parted and then rolled her over on her beam ends and cleared the deck of every moveable thing. The dories I had been working on were smashed and gone; the main boom and gaff I had been standing on were ripped clear of the mast and hanging over the lee rail. The only thing not damaged was the foresail. I was down with my feet hanging overboard and my breast against the sail.

The sea had smashed the lee bulwarks, and this saved me from going overboard. The schooner remained on her beam ends for a few seconds. The riding sail parted and she rolled back on her bottom again, with no damage done to the deck. Some water had run down the after companionway that was a little open. The men in the port bunks landed in the starboard bunks and a couple of pens of fish shifted, but no one was hurt. She was back on her bottom again with 30 fathoms of cable at her bow left out of the 90 that she was riding. Her ballast was iron slag floored down and this, with the riding sail parting, brought her back again. We cleared up the wreckage and sailed back for Gloucester with fish enough to clear expenses.

A haddock trip down on the Cape Shore

I helped rescue the crew of the schooner *Murdock* in a gale of wind one January. We had sailed from Gloucester on a haddock trip down to the Cape Shore early in December. It was a rough, cold trip. We went east as far as Liscomb on the coast of Nova Scotia, where we usually harboured and where we rode out many sou'easters. We had a few fine days and picked up a fairly good trip, lashed our boats and gear, gave her the big mainsail, as it is called, and took a fresh easterly for Gloucester.

After a run up shore to the Cape, the wind hauled to the southwest and gave us a real gale. Being in the Bay of Fundy with its high tides made the going pretty bad. We shortened down to bank sail and got ready for the worst. We head reached as the wind was southwest and, some miles from Cape Sable, we reached across for the coast of Maine all night, expecting the wind north-west in the morning. Before the sou'wester blew itself out, it came northwest and turned very cold, making matters worse. Now with only the foresail we tacked and head reached. Along the coast of Maine, perhaps 40 miles off, late in the afternoon of January 3, 1909, with wind and sea heavy, the man at the wheel sighted some miles to windward what looked like a wreck.

We set the riding sail and jib to work up under her lee to see if there was any life on board. With the glasses we could see the crew lashed in the lee rigging. After a couple of short tacks we passed under her lee. There were three men in the main rigging and two in the far rigging. Her sails had been carried away and she had a heavy list to starboard and part of her deck was under-water. When we got close, they called out, "Save us, we will sink in one hour!"

This schooner was bound from New York to Machias, Maine, with a load of hard coal. She had run into the sou'wester east of Thacher Island and lost her sails before they could take them in. Her foresail blew clear of the gaff and bolt rope and the far gaff remained hoisted. With everything loose and flying, she was a dangerous ship to get alongside. Without any sail she had drifted for two days. With her pumps choked and lying broadside to the gale, she soon began to sink.

Everything was lashed down, dories up, and the chance of saving them looked bad. I was the mate and I felt it was up to me to say if we could make it or not. The captain and many of the crew of 22 thought we might stand by, as they did not think it was fit to put a dory over, but I gave the orders and I saw to it that they were carried out. I told the captain we would work up to windward of the wreck while I got a dory ready, and if there was a man who would volunteer to go with me, I would swing out a dory and try. We made several tacks and every time we came head to wind, she went under. Nothing could be left open at that time.

The captain took the wheel and we got a windward position.

I called the men up on deck to hoist out the dory. Six men came on deck and stood by the tackle, ready to hoist her out. They had lifted the dory out on the lee rail when the captain brought her head to wind and, with a lot of headway, went under. The men at the tackle let go. Some saved themselves by jumping up on the main gaff. The man with the forward tackle was on the sheer pole and he held on to the after-dory tackle and tacked when the sea floated the dory, while the fore tackle held his at the schooner side and from the lee rail I jumped in.

The schooner did not come around, and the dory was in a fair way of jumping back on board again. My mate did not get in, so I cried out, "For God's sake, someone jump in with me!" Just then a big French fellow from Yarmouth, Nova Scotia, jumped in, and he let us go. We were very close and dead to windward of the wreck, but the wind blew so hard we could not lift our oars out of the water, but we kept head to wind and tacked down and were soon under the lee of the wreck.

The sea would break over her weather rail and wash the dory away. After several minutes under her lee, we made a dash and, as she rolled toward us, she almost filled our dory. We worked fast and the three men in the after rigging jumped in. We bailed out the dory and, in the meantime, the captain at the wheel tacked under our lee and we tried to hold her head to wind. With one man in the stern unable to move, we had no time to lose. It was bitterly cold. The schooner ranged out of our drift and he had to bring her back up close to the dory. The jib boom went over the dory, lost headway, took a sea that swept the deck, and then fell against the dory, smashing us under her bow.

I jumped and grabbed her side stays and held on to try to keep her from smashing us. The stern of the dory was knocked by the long gaff as she again rose out of the water, taking me out of the bow of the dory. When she came down, I went under, but I held on. The dory was safe alongside the schooner when she again rose out, and I was jammed between the side stays and the rail with everything gone but one rubber boot and my oilskin pants. Myself and the three men got safely on deck. This seemed to put a little spirit in the crew and they got the dory ready again. As the wind was dying out a little, two more of the crew made the second trip and saved the other two from the forward rigging.

I took over the wheel, for I knew every trick in the steering and handling of a fishing schooner. I came up to leeward of the wreck and picked up the dory from the leeside. She was hoisted on board, and the *Murdock* slowly sank beneath the waters of the Bay of Fundy.

During our rescue work another Gloucester schooner passed by; she arrived in Boston Bay 12 hours ahead of us. She reported we had a shipwrecked crew on board, as she had witnessed the return of the last dory, and gave a pencil sketch of the two schooners, which was published in the Boston papers. We made Cape Ann early on Sunday morning and found a towboat, with a doctor and first aid group, waiting for us. The crew members were taken ashore, and we were towed into Gloucester with several reporters on board.

Stories went to the papers with pictures of the schooner and crew. The pencil sketch was done by Mr. McLean, an artist in Summerville, Massachusetts, and several paintings were made from this sketch and sold to a number of the crews. We discharged our trip and were getting ready to sail again when two Carnegie officials came on board and asked all the crew of our schooner to stand in line on deck. Only 12 of the crew had been with us in the rescue. They explained that that was enough and that they were there to write up witnesses and the men who volunteered to put out the dory, and the four who took part in the rescue would get rewarded for their heroic work. The captain would receive an engraved, gold watch.

I went down and packed my old outfit for Boston and sailed on the *Lady Sybil* for Halifax, thus ending my days of fishing from the port of Gloucester.

Home again

I am reminded of John Howard Payne's lyrics from "Home! Sweet Home!": "Be it ever so humble, there's no place like home." How beautiful are those words. When I returned to Nova Scotia, I found our cottage by the lake, the one I remembered as our happy home in the country, was no more. The few members of the family that were left had moved to the city, leaving nothing but memories of bygone days.

After a month's rest with my parents, I felt the urge to find another fishing boat. I took charge of a small steam-powered craft fishing for a Scottish company in my hometown. The boat was old and not fit for business, but I picked up a crew, fitted her up, and made a few trips. I filled her full of cod and haddock and, on the way back to port, she sprang a leak. We pumped and bailed her out with buckets. The wind was coming from the southwest, and she was short of coal. On the last few miles up to the first stop where we could pick up a few bags of coal, we tore up the bunks and tables and anything that would burn, and made our passage to the dock. We discharged our load and tied up over the weekend. On Monday morning we found her lying on the bottom, decks awash.

The company decided they would build a new schooner and wanted me to take charge of her when she was finished. I decided instead to pull out of the fishing business. Within a few days I found work with the Halifax and Dartmouth ferry service. After a few months, I discovered I did not like this kind of seagoing life and went into the building trade instead. First I built myself a home and became a resident of the Town of Dartmouth. In the next few years, I built several other homes. Then came the shadow of war.

I joined the Halifax police force and was on the force when World War I was declared. I was one of the four officers to meet the first 65 people taken off a Spanish steamer by the battleship *Drake*. She had picked them up on their way to join their Allies.

They were landed at King's wharf and marched to Melville Island, a small peninsula located in the northwest arm of the Halifax harbour. I spent three weeks there as one of the guards. During the war, the Canadian government used the island to detain German and Austro-Hungarian nationals.

There were several German officers in the bunch, and they were troublesome. They wanted quarters by themselves, better food, the daily newspaper, and a bath every day. We gave them *The Herald* newspaper, but it never should have been brought into the camp as they got all the news and gave us trouble. One morning the headlines informed us of the sinking of three of our ships somewhere on the coast by a German submarine. With the deaths of nearly all on board, the commander of the submarine complained that the sinkings had been too easy and that it did not feel like war. One of the German officers, who seemed to be the chief spokesman, read aloud the notice of the deaths, and they all enjoyed a good laugh. I had placed a couple of tables across a corner of the large room that quartered them and a chair that overlooked the room. After the laugh he came over to my table and showed me the headlines. "Did you read this?" "Yes," I said. "What are we going to do to the British Navy?" he asked.

I told him to go back with his prison friends. He shook his fist in my face. I gave him my right on his right temple, and he dropped to the floor. He was slow in getting up, and then the rest of the bunch came over. My buddy, who was standing near, stepped up and, when the German came to his feet, he had a .38 staring him in the face. At the end of the week the prison was taken over by the Army, and I went back to street duty.

My first beat as a police officer was at the dry dock. I was with one sergeant and four officers. One large steamship, *Shenandoah*, was being fitted for troop service. As many as 300 men were working around the ship and the plant. The watchman at the gate had been a watchman for 15 years. A soldier was sitting down inside the gatehouse reading the morning paper when a young man wearing heavy glasses, with a pair of black overalls under his arm, gave the watchman a ticket and a cigar and a "Hello old boy," and passed through.

The officers did not seem to take much interest in their duty, so I just walked around the wall of the dock, as I could see the ship's bottom from every angle. I saw the young man again. He was leaning against a stepladder. He then carried the stepladder up to the north wall of the dock that overlooked the bottom of the ship and the men at work and levelled his lunch box from his eye to the ship's bottom and snapped a picture. After that I never lost sight of him. I called two men who were working near me and told them not to lose sight of him but not to get too close to him or interfere with his work.

They followed my orders and about one hour later he came up the ladder and walked to the head of the dock and took a picture of the deck of the ship and then went up on the end of a box car standing near and took another picture of the whole view of the dock. I was within 10 feet of him when he snapped the last picture. I took his box from him almost before he even knew I was near. For the next 30 yards I did not allow him to make one false move. I covered him with my gun and ordered him into the watch house and he placed his hands up against the wall. I searched him, removed his hardware, drove him to the station, and locked him up. He had a long criminal record and was wanted in New York and Maine, where he had failed in an attempt to blow up a bridge.

Saving the lives of many

Late in 1914, while doing boat work at the Royal Nova Scotia Yacht Squadron, we received many reports of our Royal Navy ships being sunk by enemy submarines. Ships were going down with their crew, while lifeboats and rafts remained lashed on deck. I could not understand why boats and rafts for life-saving purposes were not released automatically by the water pressure or from the bridge, before or during a sinking. After some thought and research, I decided to invent something.

Being somewhat short of money, I called a shipbuilding contractor, a sea captain of some note, the local mayor, and one of the best lawyers in Halifax. I told them I had a model of a secret patent of great value to the navy for life-saving and that if they met me at the Royal Nova Scotia Yacht Squadron I would demonstrate it. Before my demonstration, they asked me the cost of manufacturing. It had cost me less than $100. It was decided they would pay me $3 covering my work up to then, and they would form a company. They were going to patent it in England and Russia and demonstrate it in Halifax harbour. In the meantime, they got requests from several companies and the price was fixed at $1 million.

We got deeper into the war and, while men continued to struggle in the water, my patent was held up by this quickly formed company. Not till late in World War II did they give thought to my invention, simply called the Crowell device. After 17 years, the patent expired, and was taken over by somebody else. The device proved to be successful. I have a picture taken from the deck of a large oil tanker. It was published in an American magazine and explained the device's successful qualities. But I didn't receive anything more from my invention, and probably lost plenty.

I put in many hours at the Royal Nova Scotia Yacht Squadron repairing and rigging boats and yachts. One afternoon while working on a small yacht at the wharf, I heard a cry for help. I could not see the direction from which it came, so I jumped up on the pier. Out some 30 yards from the beach, a small boy was standing on a little raft. When he saw me, he cried out, "My brother is drowning down there!" I saw a little cap on the surface. In this raft they had made of driftwood and board, the brothers had paddled up the shore. As a brush of wind blew them offshore, their poorly constructed raft fell apart. Frightened, the younger one fell off the raft as it washed apart, and sank in a few seconds. He came up again but the older brother could not reach him. He had only a few minutes before the raft would have been washed from under his feet.

I lost no time in plunging from the head of the wharf. I swam to the place to which his brother pointed. His little hand came out of the water just as I reached the spot. I grabbed him and swam to shore, and found he was breathing all right. I made a second voyage and brought the other boy to shore. Several people had gathered around by this time and they took care of the two boys. I had a visit from James Power, a well-known newspaperman at the *Acadian Recorder*.

Capt. Crowell in the *Queen Mary.*

THE *QUEEN MARY*

After working through the building and repairs following the Halifax Explosion of 1917, and the end of the war, I felt the urge to move again. I went to Boston and visited a construction company. They sent me to Denville, New Jersey, on a $7 million cotton mill job. With my wife and our daughter, Helen, I spent the next two years there and learned the trade of painting and glazing on steel frames. When the mill was completed, we worked across the United States for some 10 years. From time to time I would go down to a wharf or the South Boston Yacht Club, longing for the sea.

At the club I made the acquaintance of a well-known yachting man and spent one day aboard his pleasure craft. There, while listening to the roar of the sea, I signed up to take charge of his steam yacht, which was being fitted up for a winter cruise south. I found myself yachting for the next three years. It was a steam-powered craft, 70 feet overall, built and owned by Thomas W. Lawson. We had the steam power removed and Buffalo gas engines installed. During my yachting days my wife and Helen returned to our home in Dartmouth; after three years away, I decided I would quit the sea for good, and I returned home.

The government was building new freight sheds at the South Terminals and I got a job with my tools again. But, after a few days on the job, I had a serious accident. While on the staging, I fell to the concrete floor, split my skull, and broke my left shoulder. My arm was crippled. Even after a couple of years of treatment, my arm improved little, and I was unable to work. Everything bothered me—the slightest noise or excitement. I wanted to be alone and to rest. I wanted to hear the roar of the sea again.

Day after day I would go to my workshop and sit and think of my better seagoing days. At last I thought, Why not build a small boat and sail away? At first I thought I would try the coast in the summer months. The salt water, the fresh air, and the sea spray, I believed, would help me recover. After some thought, I sketched the craft I wanted, and then made a model. I would decide later where I would sail.

Building boats wasn't new to me. I had built a few, including one that was 30 feet long. I went to work on a small ketch, with a centreboard, round bottom, 6-foot beam, and a 17-foot bottom. It was 23 feet overall, with 19 inches depth midship, a small cubby forward just big enough to crawl into, and a little bunk on the port side, with a small oil burner for heat. It would have a little afterdeck and open cockpit, 4 by 7 feet. Her under sail carried 32 yards and a square topsail, which I would use in fair and light winds. I could work only a few hours at a time, and I spent the rest of the time picturing myself sailing along. I spent many hours building this little craft, carefully cutting and fitting all the parts. I decided to sail from Newfoundland to Ireland, but I changed my mind and finally decided to sail from Canada's east coast to Canada's west coast, a voyage of more than 7,000 miles.

Many have asked me why I called my little sailboat the *Queen Mary*. I had three sisters. The youngest one, Mary, was a beautiful girl and she raised three beautiful young women, who really were queens. I called my boat *Queen Mary* after my sister. My sailboat and the transatlantic *Queen Mary* were both queens in 1936—the smallest ocean sailboat and the world's most luxurious ocean liner. I had a dream that I would cross the other *Queen Mary*'s path during my travels, but a heavy gale prevented me from giving her my report at sea.

Eventually, it was time for me to haul my own *Queen Mary* out of my workshop to fit her up with spars and rigging. I remember the first week and the many visitors and the many criticisms.

"He is going to sail away for two years, but he will never reach Vancouver in that," one said. "He is taking a dog with him; I pity the poor dog," another said.

Togo was more than a dog to me. My little pal always looked out for me. I got him during my convalescence, after my fall at the freight shed. Part cocker spaniel, he was the most intelligent animal I had ever seen. I started training him for many useful things; later I trained him to perform tricks, including high diving and playing a small piano.

Swimming, though, required no teaching. The first water he ever saw he jumped in and swam. I then taught him fishing and duck hunting. I enjoyed these sports, and he was always with me. I taught him to walk at my heel and to lie down when told. The first duck I shot I kept for a few days and I trained him to bring it to me and to find it after I had hid it.

I taught him to come when I whistled or spoke his name. The sea was nothing to him. He would dive right through the crest of a heavy sea. If I caught a fish, I killed it and gave it to him. He would carry it or swim with it to shore and leave it by the car. I could send him home with a note and he would go 2 miles and bring back what I wanted—anything that he could carry in his mouth. He would swim to my boat or shore with a card or message, and bring one back.

I taught him to swim a line to shore for me. He even learned to steer the boat by lying against the yoke. He knew the orders and he never failed me when he was on lookout. He knew danger when he saw it and was always ready to do his part. Many miles the *Queen Mary* sailed, or head reached, while I slept and Togo was on watch.

One afternoon, while fly-fishing in shoal water, I lost my fly hook. The dog had been with me, swimming back and forth. Presently I noticed him sitting on the shore; when I called him, he barked. I went over to see what his trouble was and, to my surprise, he had my fly hook. He had picked it up and known it was mine. I knew Togo had to be my companion on the *Queen Mary*.

At last I launched my *Queen Mary* from the pier in Dartmouth and got her under way. Everything was handled from where I stood at the companionway: all halyards, downhauls, anchor and sea anchor, sheets, and every bit of running gear. An 8-foot stick with a knife and a hook on the end is well worth carrying aboard any boat. From where I stood, I could cut or untie anything forward or aft. The boat, when ballasted to the waterline, carried 200 pounds of ballast. Just a little bit under the correct ballast weight, it saved her from sinking several times.

The boat had a double bottom: the inner was 1¼ inches thick with a bevelled bottom; the outer 1¾ inches thick overlapping the garboard nailing, fastened through with brass screw bolts staggered every 6 inches. The stem was of yellow birch and its spoon bow cut. The stern was also yellow birch, 2½ feet from the top of the garboard to the stern juniper knee. Her timbers were of ¾ by 1½ inch hackmatack, a material used in the construction of wooden ships; they were very light but close together. The planking was ¾ inches thick with native white pine planked with 10 streaks a side and copper fastened to the waterline. All the material used in this boat was as light as possible.

Many advised me to use heavier material, knowing the tremendous pounding by the seas that this little craft would receive. But I had different ideas. Everything was to be strong, but light, including the spars and the rigging. When people looked down on its deck, they often thought it was far too frail, but I built it to suit myself.

A trial run

I found the *Queen Mary* slow during my first sea trial. The centreboard was too light, and she was a little down by the bow. My 24-pound dog was forward, but when I called him aft, I noticed the change, and found that she trimmed aft. I thought the

Queen Mary would be the smallest boat to undertake this long voyage and knew that the responsibility would be great. But I told myself I would never turn back as others did. I prayed to God to help me.

My steering gear from the rudder post came up through to the deck and had a yoke, a piece of 2-inch pipe, split open within 3 inches of the end. This end fitted over the rudder head and a bolt through secured it safely, making a safe and neat job. I made a light ash rod about 8 feet long properly stickled at the end of the yoke, which reached to my companionway. It operated from fore to aft and proved itself very serviceable, as I could use my hand or foot from any angle.

As July 16, 1936, drew near, I began to fit out for my long voyage to Vancouver. I planned to be gone two years. News of my voyage travelled, and the press became interested. Many reporters came to talk with me. I remember one particular visit from a female writer who wished to accompany me and help with expenses. At that time I did not have the boat rigged, and she thought the *Queen Mary* was my tender. I said, "No, this is the ship that's going to carry me around for the next two years." "Oh, dear, this is only a rowboat. Where am I going to sleep?" she asked. "Do not worry, old dear," I said. "I am sailing alone and have no room for passengers. I feel this is going to be the smallest sailboat on the longest coastline passage ever made."

Newspapermen came from the Halifax papers. I expected to get some money for my stories or reports that I would send during my long voyage. I was a well-known seaman. One of the Halifax papers had carried many reports of me over the past 30 years, but they did not offer me a cent, nothing but publicity. I could not live on that. They wanted my life story and pictures of me, my dog, and my boat—for nothing.

Before I left, I had a wonderful surprise. I found a wheelbarrow full of canned goods, jam, milk, and other supplies from my friends in the neighbourhood. I was now properly fitted out.

Capt. Crowell and Togo on the *Queen Mary*.

FROM HALIFAX TO VANCOUVER IN 14 MONTHS

As I sailed from Dartmouth on July 16, 1936, with a bon voyage cry from at least 1,000 people, I believed that my craft, as small as she was, would carry me to Vancouver. While lying at anchor for a few minutes I looked her over and spoke to Togo, my sole companion, as this was his first trip under sail. I showed him his quarters in the afterdeck.

I had given this voyage every thought and I knew the responsibility and the dangers I would have to endure. I bade my friends and family goodbye, dipped my flag, and sailed out of Halifax harbour. Togo barked his goodbye to the parting crowd.

Sailing for my first port, Indian Harbour, the wind was light and I had time for thought. I had only $40. The only chance I had of earning more was through the hospitality of the people in my ports of call. I thought of what lay ahead for me and my boat—rough seas, long cold nights, gales and fog, thunder and lightning, and the long sail in the Pacific Ocean.

At least I had lots of food. After about 10 miles I spoke to a fishing boat and the captain gave me a fresh mackerel. As the *Queen* drifted along, I prepared my first meal at sea. Togo sat near me on the washboard and watched every move I made. He did not like fish very much, but I had some bones for him. We both enjoyed our dinner. As I sailed along the long coastline, I caught a lot of fish. When I said "fish for dinner today, Togo," he moved away, but if I said "meat," he came near and lifted his ears.

July 17–19. Make Indian Harbour at 7 p.m. Distance 35 miles. Remain at Indian Harbour over the weekend. Stow away stores and gear. Clean up boat. Meet old friends. Spend Sunday visiting and going to church with the mayor of Indian Harbour. At church they sing a farewell hymn, "Let Your Lower Lights Be Burning," and pray for the success of my sailing. On Sunday afternoon many of the people gather down at the wharf to give my little boat the once-over. She lay there, proudly flying her flags and decorations. Togo does some high diving from the government shed on the pier from a height of 20 feet.

The South Shore to Yarmouth

On the morning of July 20, a neighbourhood crowd came down to the wharf to see me sail. They gave me bottles of strawberry jam and fruit from their gardens. Along with many kisses from the women and a handshake from Warden Covey, I sailed with a "cheerio." The wind was from the northeast but very light on a course across the bay. Sailing distance 18 miles.

July 21. Get under way at 6 a.m. Wind light. Head work all day. At 3 p.m., calm. At 4 p.m., light air. One mile south from Cross Island. Pick up a light breeze and make Dublin Shore. Anchor at Hirtle's Flow at 7:30. Sailing distance 22 miles.

July 22. My birthday. I am 56 years young. Get under way at 5 a.m. Wind light and northeast. Course, west by south. At 7:30 a.m., making about 3 miles per hour. Find many fishing along my course. All seem to know me, and give me many fish. Wind breezes up at 10 a.m. Still on course. Make Liverpool at 3:30 p.m. Sailing distance 30 miles. Pick up first news from home.

July 23. Tie up at the government pier at Brooklyn. Friends drive down to the pier to see me sail. They give me oranges and many nice things. Cast off my line. They also wish me bon voyage. Wind southwest and no course. Head work till dark. No harbour, so I stand south till 10 p.m. Tack and stand on the land till 3:30 a.m.

Thick fog. Wind southwest. First night out. Sound and find 8 fathoms of water. I have made about 15 miles. Tack and stand south again.

July 24. Wind still southwest. Fog very thick. Stand south two hours. Tack and stand in again on the land. Heading northwest by west. I am 10 miles southwest of Port Mouton or 15 miles south east of Lockeport. Noon. Wind hauled south.

July 30. After a week's sail, drifting light winds, and fog, I make it to Yarmouth. I drop a bottle with my ship's name and date. In Yarmouth, I meet the government boat *Acadia*, and Captain Hawes at the Yarmouth steamship pier. I go aboard for dinner.

Find out they are celebrating "Old Home Week," Yarmouth's 275th anniversary. Captain Fry of the fire department and a newspaper reporter come to the *Queen Mary*. They ask me to speak on the radio and my dog to perform for children at the exhibition grounds. We agree. In the evening Togo also performs for the firemen. At midnight we call it a night.

July 31. Easterly gales. Spend August 1 and 2 in Yarmouth.

August 3. Wash up boat and take in supplies. Talk with Captain Cousen on the government boat *Canadian*. Get under way at noon and sail west. Make Port Maitland. Tie up at government wharf. Sailing distance 15 miles. Spend our last night in Nova Scotia. After meeting friends and waiting for favourable winds, I clear for Gloucester, with a light easterly and thick fog.

American waters

August 4. Under way at 4:30 a.m. Fresh breeze southeast. Cross the Bay of Fundy, 10:30 a.m., light gale blowing. Topsail set, making 6 miles per hour. At 6:30 p.m., I sight Grand Manan Island, the largest of the islands in the Bay of Fundy. It was once visited by the likes of explorer Samuel de Champlain and pirate William "Captain" Kidd. I make the coast of Maine at 9:30 p.m. Wind comes off northwest. Thunder and lightning. Anchor under land somewhat sheltered. Sailing distance 70 miles.

August 5. American customs boat approaches me wanting to know if all is well aboard. Wind comes fresh southwest and tide runs in very strong. Go in to Bailey's Mistake, 20 miles west of Eastport.

August 6. Wind southwest and light. Sail 20 miles. Anchor in small cove.

August 7. Sailing for Portland. Calm all day.

August 8. Get under way, light air south, thick of fog. At 11 a.m., wind draws east. Fog very thick and tide running in the bay. At 2:30 p.m., pick up fog alarm and fairway buoy at Jonesport. Go in and pick up letters. Fill water kegs and speak to customs. Find it to be Snug Harbour, home to mostly fishermen. Remain only for one hour. Fog still very thick, making navigation difficult. It is dangerous along the coast. But I get out and sail all night.

August 9. Fog clears. At 10:30 p.m., made about 40 miles. Wind now northwest. Close haul. At 12 a.m., I sight Mount Desert and sail on toward Bakers Island. Get near west end of Bakers Island and spend the night. Sailing distance 15 miles.

August 10. Speak to lighthouse keeper, who is hauling traps. At 8 a.m., the wind is very light. He kindly gives me seven small lobsters. Get a good breeze northeast and set topsail. At 10:30 a.m., wind draws north and brings a squall with snow. Thunder and lightning. Douse all sails except jib, and haul in northwest. At 4:30 p.m., I sight land. Wind moderates and again set sails. Anchor at

8 p.m. Sailing distance 35 miles. They send a boat out for me to come ashore. This is a small island off the coast of Maine with a small harbour on the northwest side. The people there heard my radio report and give me the hall for Togo to perform. We give a concert.

August 11. Togo does a high dive from the wharf and entertains some 60 people from Boothbay Harbour, Maine. Get under way. Wind very light. Anchor at low point. By 9 p.m., have sailed 20 miles. Speak to no one on this trip. Now about 25 miles from Portland.

Before we left on our voyage, I had trained Togo not only to do useful things but also tricks. He entertained thousands while visiting ports of call. The training took a lot of time and patience but, after two years, he entertained at schools, hospitals, and theatres, and for Boy Scouts and many private entertainment engagements and Army and Navy functions. At one gathering he entertained 1,200 children for one and a half hours. Togo wore three uniforms, but his best was that of a nurse, and he had five main acts.

No. 1: On a special piano Togo played the tune "My dog, Touser." The piano was 3 feet long and inches high. It was a real piano, not a toy. He had a proper stool and sat up and played to the motion of my moving hands. This was his opening act.

No. 2: Dressed as a nurse, Togo picked up a little doll, dressed as a baby, from a chair. When I gave him the order, he walked on his hind legs and carefully placed the doll in a carriage and with his forepaws wheeled it across the stage. He then picked it up in his mouth and gave it to a lady sitting on a chair at the end of the stage. I then ordered him to take the baby from the lady and put it in the carriage and bring it back to me. After that, he got up on his little chair and waited for my next order. I took the same doll and placed it in a dollhouse just large enough for him to enter on a 6-foot-high stepladder. I placed the doll inside the house with

Togo and his tricks: carrying a British flag (left) and playing a tiny piano (right).

the doors closed, facing the audience. When I was ready, I turned on a light and told him that the house was on fire and to go and save the baby. He went up the ladder, picked up the doll with his mouth, and with his head pushed open the doors, and jumped down in my arms with the doll.

No. 3: Togo performed three different ways with a large drum. He first spun the drum—this was done by a bar through the centre of the drum operated from a stand—at great speed while balancing on top and stopped it at my order and went the opposite way. Finally I pulled out the bar and he got on top and rolled it around the stage while balancing on top.

No. 4: Wearing a sailor's uniform, Togo paraded across the stage holding a British or American flag in his mouth. A cleat on the end of the flagstaff brought the flag directly over his head. In this act I took part with a musket on my back and, to the tune of some fast music, he danced a reel with me.

No. 5: In the dressing room I showed Togo where he would find the articles I wanted him to get for me in the performance. I put on the floor my slippers, a book, a ball, a newspaper, and my hat. He knew where to find them. Then during the performance I sat on a chair, called him over, and said, "Togo, get my slippers." He brought them to me. If I called the orders right, he never made a mistake.

Togo had other tricks. Wearing a special suit and bonnet he impersonated American actress Mae West. He took short steps with a little handbag perched on his forepaw. This was a cute trick. He also walked like a flapper. He changed over to a hop and, as the tight skirt required a short step, he did it with a little hop; then he did the two-step in and out between my legs. He performed through a hoop, did somersaults, and acted with me as Daniel Boone and his dog. I had him go under a bush that was placed on the stage and he brought me out a rabbit.

Togo's high dive was an outdoor trick and always drew a big crowd. I had three light extension ladders, 20 feet high with a diving platform at the top. He stood on the platform. When I was preparing him for his dive, I would count to three and throw a rubber ball, and he picked it up and swam with it to a nearby float or boat.

Portland, Maine

August 12. Get under way at 6 a.m. Fair wind across Newcastle Bay to west shore. At 12:30, speak to a lobster fisherman. Tide very strong. Tie up at Portland State pier at 4 p.m. Crowd comes down and makes us feel welcome. Get badly needed fresh supplies and meet some lobster fishermen. Sailing distance 16 miles. Give news to reporters. Cook a large steak and onions. Write in my logbook and settle down for a good night's sleep.

August 13. Sleep most of the day. In the afternoon many come to see the boat.

August 14–15. Meet friends from home and they take me to their home to spend the evening. Go to customs, get sailing licence, and drive through Portland. Take in water and supplies.

August 16. Set sail. It has been thick of fog for three days. Tide fair and wind light. Make 15 miles and anchor in a cove east of Cape Elizabeth at 7 p.m. A boat comes by and asks me to go ashore and have supper. I spend the evening with these fine people.

August 17. Under way 6 a.m. Good breeze. Head work all day. At 4 p.m., we sail west till dark. Wind north by east. Anchor in a little cove near a lighthouse, called Bennett's Pool. Sailing distance 40 miles.

August 18. Get under way at 6 a.m. About 15 miles from Old Orchard Beach, Maine, located on the inner side of Saco Bay. It is a popular beach spot. With the sun shining again, I change my sailing plans and call in there. As I sail in by the end of the plank wharf, I see a flag of welcome, but the seas are so heavy that I cannot land my *Queen Mary*. I give my mate, Togo, his first message card, and overboard he goes. He swims through the breakers to the beach to meet hundreds of people. The lifeguards take the message and give him one in return. He swims back and I lift him on board. The message reads, "Another lifeguard coming out." In a few minutes I am on my way to shore. The time is 11 a.m. Togo proves that he is a trustworthy messenger. We entertain a crowd till dark, doing all our best tricks. We also sell cards and pamphlets to raise a little money for our trip, and then take a swim in the surf. We say goodbye and they return us to the *Queen Mary* with a letter of goodwill and bon voyage, along with a nice bit of expense money.

August 19. Get under way at 6 a.m. Wind north. Very dark. Catch up with bad thunderstorm and run through this wind and rain.

Noon, clears. Wind north. Anchor in People's Pool. Now 10 miles east of Portsmouth. Sail 12 more miles.

August 20. Get under way again. Wind northeast. Set all sail, topsail. At 2 p.m., wind moderates. Sight Thacher Island, 12 miles east of the Gloucester light. Air light. Get in and anchor at Rock Point, 3 miles east of Thacher Island. Lifeguard rows me ashore.

Gloucester, Massachusetts

August 21. Get under way at 6 a.m. Light air, north. Pass in through narrows. Stiff breeze west. Head work up through toward Cape Ann. Make Gloucester harbour at 2 p.m.

August 22. Clean up boat. Go to post office and pick up mail, and go to city hall. Meet the mayor of Gloucester and all the council. All fine fellows. Go out to lunch with them and meet many friends.

August 23. Mayor gives me city hall to entertain with Togo.

August 24. At 2:30 p.m., Togo performs at city hall for the children. At 7:30 p.m., Togo entertains at Fisherman's Bethel. Have a large crowd.

August 25. Now lying at Chipman's wharf. Meet several friends and also some shipmates from 30 years ago. Money earned in Gloucester, $6.

August 26. Southeast gale. A newspaper reporter and his wife come on board for a story and to take pictures. They try to repair my camera, which had been filled with water. At 1 p.m., I get under way for Boston. Wind ahead. No course. Make 7 miles. Calm. No harbour.

Boston, Massachusetts

August 27. Make course to Boston. Make narrows at 12 noon. Wind west. Heading near to the wind up the harbour. Have a fair tide. Make fish pier at Boston at 4 p.m. An army of pressmen crowd around my boat.

August 28. Go to State House and meet Governor James Curley. He gives me a warm handshake and says that all good seamen sail into Boston harbour; calls in five or six Nova Scotians and introduces them. Share a few stories and go out for supper. Go to Seamen's Institute and answer letters and send cards to friends. It is now 7 p.m.

August 29. Go back to Boston and call the *Boston Globe* newspaper office and meet the editor. He gives me $5 for a story. We go in to the house where Paul Revere once lived and look over many things from his era. Mr. Revere was an American silversmith, engraver, early industrialist, and patriot of the American Revolution. Go down to wharf. Fill water kegs and take in supplies. Write letters and cards and turn in at 10:30 p.m. Weather has been fine with light west winds.

Cape Cod Canal

August 30. Get under way at 7 a.m. Wind fair. Sail out of Boston harbour and set course for Cape Cod Canal, 52 miles. Wind very light. Many pleasure craft and small boats in the bay. Boil some corned beef and have dinner at 1 p.m. Have sailed about 25 miles. Wind freshening up. Course southwest by west. Take in topsail. Wind hauling to the south at 6:30 p.m. Now 10 miles from the canal. Wind very light at 10:30 p.m. Anchor near entrance and sleep till morning.

August 31. Row in to canal at 6 a.m. Tide now running through to the south. Speak to pilot boat and start going with the tide. Distance through about 9 miles. Pleasure boats, steamers, and submarines all coming north. Construction work going on at both sides of canal—widening, straightening, and cutting out shoal ground. This canal has been of great assistance to small craft, for many a hard battle has been fought rounding the light and Cape Cod. Man at gate calls out asking the dimensions of my boat. When he finds out where I'm from, he says, "Halifax is my home town." Get out in the bay and realize it took me three hours to come through. Hoist sails and find wind west and very light. Still have fair tide. I am now at Good Island and find they are changing the entrance, dredging through a small island and making a straighter entrance. Westerly wind freshening up. Set topsail. At 11 a.m., east of New Bedford. Make perhaps 5 miles per hour. Make a cup of tea and have lunch. Now 1 p.m. Weather fine. Wind hauled northeast. Wind fair all day. Make a small cove east of Newport. Go ashore to a small island where some buildings have been torn down. Old lighthouse has been removed. Good place for a night's sleep. Togo goes ashore for a run, and we have supper. And then I haul offshore and anchor. Now 8:30 p.m.

September 1. I wake up to find a light breeze from the south and thick of fog. Get breakfast. Speak to a couple of fishermen in a small boat. I am about 10 miles west of Fall River. Wind still coming from the south and the weather is bad. Haul in and make poor anchorage, 10 a.m. Lay there in shelter from the rain and wind storm. A boat rows out from a nearby island and gives me two small fish. Decide to get under way. I pull out the main mast. Ship long tiller. Cover cockpit and set foresail. Newport is now 14 miles. Heavy sea. Wind a gale and tide ahead and the sea is very rough. I know now I should not have left the protection of the island. At 1:30 p.m., sight the lightship off Newport. Keep off northwest. Still 5 miles from shelter. Rain eases. Visibility about 3 miles. Sight what looks to be a fishing boat smashing against a ledge on the coast. Would like to help but know I am lucky to be afloat myself. I wouldn't be much help. Heavy sea smashes over the boat which breaks canvas over the cockpit. Second sea comes on board and fills her full from end to end. Too far inside of red buoy. Seas breaking on shoal water. She runs with seas dead aft and I bail out with a large bucket. I remain afloat. I get in smoother water and anchor under eastern land in a little cove under eastern shore. I'm glad this day is over.

Newport, Rhode Island

September 2. Go up to the fish pier. Get the boat dried and some hot food. I get a report from Eagle Island that a boat was lost with two men. Lifeguard saved one man. I regret that I could not go to their assistance, although I saw the distress signal. It is 9 a.m. and the *Queen Mary* lies very comfortably tied to the fish pier.

September 3. Crowds come down to see the *Queen Mary* at the fish pier and watch Togo do tricks. Manager takes me for a drive through Newport and we visit the fish market, which has about 700 cash customers. People pass through and buy cards of the *Queen Mary*. It is now 9 p.m. Will stay here for Labour Day.

September 4. It is a fine morning. At 8:30 a.m., I have breakfast and meet Wilbur Wright, who, along with his brother Orville, is credited for inventing and building the first successful airplane. He asks me to visit him in Florida. I also meet the commander of the Navy yard. Have many visitors. At 10 p.m., the moon is shining in the companionway. It is a glorious night.

September 5. Visit crippled children's hospital and camp.

September 6. Togo goes to the local hospital and entertains 60 children. At 4 p.m., wind southeast. Heavy. Travel down the harbour and anchor in small cove east side. Sailing distance 5 miles.

New Haven, Connecticut

September 7. Get under way at 6 a.m. Head work all day. Light southwest. Make 30 miles. Speak to fishermen from Point Judith, dragging for flounders. They give me a mess of fresh fish. Anchor under Judith light. Sailing distance 38 miles.

September 8. Get under way at daybreak. Light wind, northwest, and fair tide. Round Judith Point and steer course west. At 9:30 a.m., wind hauls out southeast. Set topsail. Making about 5 miles per hour. Now about 10 miles east of New London, Connecticut. Visibility very bad. Will soon enter Long Island Sound. There's a gale coming. I sight a small power boat. Course west by north. At 1 p.m., I have an unexpected visitor—a yellow bird comes aboard. It looks very tired. After resting awhile, it catches a fly, which seems to revive it. It chirps and sings me a little song before flying for land. Wind breezes up. Visibility better. I enter Long Island Sound. Pass first fairway buoy. Pass Mason Island. Fair wind and fair tide. Now 10 miles west of New London. Anchor in small cove and have supper. Now 7:30 p.m. Sailing distance probably 25 miles.

September 9. I get under way with a fair wind. Sail till 9:30 a.m. Tide turns and runs east. Tie up at summer beach and go ashore. There I meet about 30 people. That's all that are left of the hundreds that spent the summer season there. Nice wharf. Togo plays the piano and does some tricks; we get $5, a new watch, and a leather pouch to carry it in. A fine lot of people. Three hours and the tide turns, so I get under way at 4:30 p.m., light wind southwest. Lay course along west north. It's now dark. Pick up fairway lights and run into small breakwater and anchor with a fleet of yachts. I find out this is Angel Head Bay. There's a big yacht club here and many summer homes. Sailing distance 15 miles.

September 10. Get under way at 4:30 a.m. The wind is from the northeast, but very light by noon. Head work till 4:30 p.m., when I make New Haven. Wind breezing up. Pick up a race with two yachts bound for Stratford, Connecticut. Wind getting very heavy. Head work. I get close to one yacht. Sail a little faster and stand up better than the yacht as she has a very small spread of sail.

My first bad storm

Hoping to catch up with the RMS *Queen Mary* on the night of September 17, I anchor in Stratford. I come inside of the break-water hoping for an early start, but the weather is bad. It's blowing up from the southeast. Early the next morning I get under way. I have to make two short tacks to get out, but I run against a bank and lose the centreboard chain down through the box. This delays me two hours. I pull out in deep water, anchor, and put a strap around the centreboard underneath the boat and haul it back into the box. I can't get it far enough to put the chain on, so I saw 6 inches off the side of the box. Reef heavy copper wire through and haul it through in place. It is 9:30 a.m. and a gale is blowing 30 miles per hour. Storm warnings along the coast. But I haul out in the sound and prepare for a long run. Pull the main mast out and lash everything down. Double reef the foresail. Ship long tiller and steer from the companionway. Boat completely covered.

Wind increases. Heavy squall and very rough. By 11 a.m., it is blowing perhaps 50 miles per hour. I am probably moving 7 miles per hour. Wind northeast, almost dead aft. At 1 p.m., wind probably 60 miles per hour. *Queen Mary* running beautifully. No water coming over cockpit. Sea terribly heavy. Visibility poor. At 3 p.m., wind still increasing, probably to 80 miles per hour. I let the fore-sail run down to the deck. The hollow of the seas brings the crest to the top of my spars, 17 feet. It is almost unbelievable that I am still running off this gale. Visibility now better. Sight many craft lying in shelter under a small island on the west side. Sea very heavy and tide running to windward. Situation looks bad. Pass small craft with spar broken off and decks awash. I know I have to make shelter if possible. Sight cape in the distance and haul over to western land. The seas are far heavier than any I ever saw in all my years of fishing on the Banks off Newfoundland. It is 4:30 p.m.

I want to make harbour at Grey Head. The wind is still increasing. The *Queen Mary* climbs over walls of water that I thought couldn't be done by such a small craft. It is getting dark and I sight a red buoy off a small island, which I leave very close on starboard bow. Boat now heading southwest by west. I haul up west and pass a fairway buoy. Hard to believe that I could get in there. I can see nothing but one mass of breakers. Make it in over shoal water and what I thought was a breakwater. See the yards of a square-rigged ship. Round up close to the end of a wharf and throw the loop over first shot. Haul away from the wharf, drop anchor, and lie somewhat heading to sea. I feel satisfied that I made shelter. It is very dark and thundering heavily. At 8:30 p.m., the wind jumps off from the north without warning and it rains terrifically. I am awake most of the night in the cockpit, bailing and shoving logs and boat wreckage of every imaginable description. After a while I get another line to the wharf. I feel as if every minute could be my last one. It is the longest and hardest night of my voyage so far.

September 19. 3:30 a.m. I have been wet since 9 a.m. yesterday. I go below. I can't find one dry place on board. At last I discover one dry match and light a piece of rag soaked in kerosene oil. I light my little oil stove and make some coffee. After two hours sleep, daylight finds me 12 miles east of Ward Island, New York. I get under way with a light breeze northwest. I tie up at Ward Island at 9:30 a.m. and wait for a fair tide to go under the bridge. At noon, I get a fair tide and go through to Bellevue Hospital pier. After drying out, I have one of the best night's sleep ever.

New York City, New York

September 20. I go to the New York Yacht Club and learn I still have two days before the arrival of the great *Queen Mary*. I made

The two *Queen Mary*s in New York City.

a record run of more than 70 miles. After being photographed and recounting stories to various papers, I meet a Captain Lewis of the Yacht Club and am welcomed at a gathering around my little *Queen Mary*.

September 21. 8 a.m. During breakfast I meet the caretaker of the club, who presents me with the club's flags. Captain Lewis gives me an anchor, among other useful things. In the early morning, I sail around the city waterfront to find the great *Queen Mary*. She has arrived. Together at the pier we are the greatest steamship in the world and the smallest ocean sailboat. Thousands crowd the pier to see us. When I pull in alongside this great ship, Sir Edgar T. Britten, the captain, sends for me to come on board. He had received a message to look out for a small sailboat, called the *Queen Mary*, at sea off Sandy Hook, New York.

They arrange for a man to take care of my boat, which they tie up alongside the great *Queen Mary*. On board, I am introduced to Sir Britten, and the next day I receive visitors at the companionway. Late in the afternoon of the second day, I present to this great man a package of tea from Howard Wentzell, of Halifax. Sir Britten credited me for sailing the smallest sailboat in the world in what he considered the worst storm in his more than 40 years of sailing.

After looking over my little *Queen Mary*, he said, "I cannot believe my own eyes, but I knew you were there and that little sailboat was manned by a seaman of no mean ability." Then he took me to the control room and explained the navigational instruments. He also made arrangements for me to have tea on the morning before he sailed and presented me with a bronze crest of the two ships. It was made from a piece of metal from the ship's doorplate, in remembrance of the trip we made. He also gave me a signed letter calling us friends and brothers to all our seagoing ancestors. He had the boatswain give me rope and whatever else I wanted for my little ship. The last day at the bow of the *Queen Mary* was a busy one; thousands of people passed my little *Queen Mary* and I answered countless questions.

September 28. A drive through New York City. Visit post office and customs. Pick up letters and mail from home. In the afternoon, I entertain children at the clubhouse and then spend the evening writing and talking with friends.

September 29. A welcoming fresh breeze coming from the northeast. Although it is ladies' night at the yacht club, they are preparing a big night for me. I had planned to sail this morning but I've been asked to stay over. I meet the reporter for the club and he writes a story. It is the closing night of the season. I join the party at 8:30 p.m. and find about 60 couples there. Togo and I put on our act at 9 p.m. and receive $7. We stay till the party ends at about 2 a.m.

September 30. Weather bad and raining. Wind southeast. Decide to stay put and spend the day in the luxury of the clubhouse. Do some writing and have dinner with F.C. Cameron, who made a 1,700-mile trip to Chicago through the Great Lakes in a small outboard boat with a speed of 22 miles per hour. Early the next morning I take in my ship's stores and sail out of New York, waving to the Statue of Liberty. I round Sandy Hook and, with a fair breeze, sail south and out of sight of the Big Apple. The wind breezes up and I harbour at Camden Point. I prepare my supper while my little pal lies down for a good night's sleep.

The Atlantic City coast

October 1. Make it down the coast. Sail from Atlantic City at 9 a.m. Weather bad and very rough. Wind is coming from the north and is heavy. I sight a motorboat with a distress signal up. I can't make it to her on account of the tide and high sea. The lifeguard should get to them any minute. At 11 a.m., I sail away, but they are still at anchor among the breakers. I am sailing south along the Atlantic City coast. Thirty-seven years ago, I rode a bad storm 17 miles to anchor off this coast in the four-masted schooner *Maude Palmer*. I never will forget the seas in that gale. Two ships drove ashore, one of them a sister ship to the *Maude Palmer*. Wind hauls west and I have head work along this coast. Work to windward all day. Have a fair tide. Anchor on the coast. At 8:30 p.m., sailing distance 30 miles. Wind dies out. The moon rises and shines over the Atlantic in all its glory.

October 2. Find a light air springing up and I get under way at 3 a.m. At 9 a.m., I sight Cape May. Wind breezes up southeast. At 1 p.m., about 3 miles south of Cape May, I throw a large bottle overboard with a note bearing my position. I cross Delaware Bay. A breeze from the northwest makes the going very bad. I take in mainsail and jog under foresail and sail about 20 miles. It is now very rough. Wind on starboard bow. Sea very heavy. At 5 p.m., almost out of sight of land. Getting dark. Sailing distance 40 miles. I expect a bad night. My lantern will not stay lit. Midnight, close her up and turn in for sleep. Wind very heavy, west by north.

Chesapeake Bay

October 3. Glad to see daylight. Wind hauls northeast. I decide to go through the canal and into Chesapeake Bay. Have a good run up Delaware Bay to the Delaware River. Wind moderates. I anchor, as the tide is very strong. At 2:30 p.m., I turn in for badly needed sleep. At 6 p.m., I get under way again. Wind light northeast. Speak to a large yacht coming out from the canal. They tell me it is still 35 miles to go to the canal. Midnight. Tide turns again, and I anchor. After a hot coffee, I sleep till morning.

October 4. 7 a.m. Sailing distance 20 miles. Go on board a large dredge working on the inland canal. 12 a.m., have dinner with these boys. Take some pictures of the crew. They give me some bacon and eggs and Togo gets some fresh meat. Tide with me, wind light, and I make about 10 miles. I get in the canal at 1:30. The tide is fair and I pass under the first bridge going west to Chesapeake Bay, an estuary lying inland from the Atlantic, surrounded by Maryland and Virginia. Haul over to avoid a large Norwegian steamer coming around the narrows. Mud scow close behind a large power yacht, which should pass me on the port side, but does not. He drives me ashore in the heavy tide. Togo jumps off on the scow, but I save him. I receive a bad jam between the yacht and scow but find the *Queen Mary* not hurt except for my lifeline; it has been stripped off and is hanging astern. Underneath fifth bridge. It is dark. I tie up at the side of the canal and cook myself a meal of bacon, fresh tomatoes, fried potatoes with salad dressing, and fresh peaches for dessert. My first meal since 7 a.m. Sailing distance 30 miles.

BOUND FOR HOLLYWOOD IN 23-FOOT KETCH

Aboard the ketch Queen Mary, 23 feet long, Capt. William H. Crowell, bound from Halifax, N. S., to Hollywood, is shown as he arrived in Baltimore with Togo, his sole companion on the 17,000-mile trip. Crowell hopes to crash the movies. (Associated Press Photo)

The Cornell Daily Sun, October 6, 1936.

Baltimore, Maryland

October 5. The canal is 14 miles long and has 12 miles of narrows. This lets me out in Chesapeake Bay. I've got no wind, but the tide is going with me. I pick up a light breeze to the northeast. It is 50 miles to North Point, off Baltimore. At 9 a.m., the wind is breezing up. Making about 5 miles per hour. Wind still breezing up. At 3 p.m., I have a sandwich and a bottle of root beer at the tiller. Making about 6 miles per hour when I sight light off Baltimore. The wind is dying out and I still have 8 miles to go. No wind. Calm. Put up small light and turn in. About one hour's sleep when Togo flies onto the deck and starts barking. The light has gone out, and a large towboat smashes into the side of the *Queen Mary*. I grab a line and jump on board. He calls out, "Where are your lights?" He tows me in, and I tie up at Maryland Yacht Club.

October 6. I'm among some 500 boats. They give me the key to the club, where I meet the officials, including the fleet captain. Togo gives them a few tricks and they make arrangements for a party in the evening. I also get an invitation from the mayor. I make many friends here. They all give me something, whether it be rope or paint for my boat. I don't stay long in the club. I have to repair my boat from the damages caused by the towboat in the bay.

Annapolis, Maryland

Spend some days in Annapolis, the capital of Maryland and the home of the midshipmen of America. A midshipman is an officer cadet or commissioned officer of junior rank in the Navy. There are 2,200 boys in training here.

October 10. Beautiful and warm. I do some work on my boat putting in a new lifeline and halyards. A kind lady arrives with a basket of food for me, and bones and canned food for Togo, after reading a story about us in the local paper. At noon, she drives me uptown to sightsee. I have supper at the yacht club and give a talk, which I am told is interesting.

October 11. I go to the club and do some writing. The wind is north, and I want to get away today, but am to entertain some Sunday school children. Togo plays for them and seems to enjoy their presence. At 1 p.m., I bid the party goodbye and sail down the coast. At 9 p.m., I anchor behind a breakwater after a 3-mile sailing distance.

October 12. Get under way at daylight. Wind northwest. Steer south. Get breakfast while the *Queen Mary* reaches along. The sea is smooth. Wind now breezes up hard and the going gets bad. At 11 a.m., the seas are very heavy. Wind aft the beam. I cannot leave the tiller. At 2:30 p.m., wind hauls more westerly. Too rough to sail. Let off main sheet and the *Queen Mary* jogs under foresail, making a south course. I can tell it's going to be a bad night. I'm probably 120 miles north of Norfolk. Take in jib and mainsail and reef foresail and prepare for a bad night. Midnight, tack and head reach in northwest.

October 13. Everything is wet on board. Not looking forward to the day ahead. Wind moves to the northeast and I haul in to Cove Point light. Togo swims ashore with a card. I tack and pick him up again and find he has a message for me: "Please come ashore, we want to talk with you." I tack and land the boat on the beach. I find the lighthouse keeper and his wife. They give me a basket of apples and doughnuts and some shark's teeth for souvenirs. I push off and get on course, southwest. I cross Washington Bay, with the wind very heavy. Ease off the foresheet in a very heavy squall. Making probably 6 miles per hour. At 5 p.m., wind moderating and haul more northwest. Haul in on the land and anchor near beach. One of my best day's run, about 60 miles. At 8:30 p.m., my day ends.

October 14. 3:30 a.m. Wind breezes up to the northeast and I have to get under way. It is getting rough. I haul off land. It is dark. The water is now 12 feet deep. I ship some heavy seas, which break and almost fill the cockpit, but I clear and ease off the sheet. I sight a gas buoy and steer off 5 miles. Wind breaks in northeast, bringing rain and fog. It is probably blowing 30 miles an hour. Here I have to heave to under foresail. The boat is head reaching south. At 10 a.m., the seas are very heavy. Fills out main mast. Ship long tiller and cover cockpit. At 2 p.m., wind still heavy. Keep off and try to harbour at Newport News. Run in toward western land. It's a bad thing to do, but I am taking a chance. Fog thick and wind hauls south and I make land on almost the right spot, for which I had set my course. I tie up alongside two fishing boats in a small cove. It is now 9:30 p.m. Sailing distance about 28 miles. Finally, I can have a good rest.

October 15. In the morning I find that I am in a small cove in the mouth of Newport News, about 30 miles north of Norfolk. Get under way at 7:30. Light wind northeast but very rough, as there is a shoal. At 9 a.m., the wind is strong and hauls again to the south. Tide coming out of Newport News harbour and wind breezes up hard to the south. Boat washing very badly, but must carry on. Wind hauls back to the east a little, probably just in time to save me from being lost. Three more miles and then I will be able to keep off. The situation now looks a little better. Clean shoal point and keep off. Arrive at Norfolk late in the evening and tie up at the end of a pier. Light a fire to get warm. Sailed probably 35 miles.

Norfolk, Virginia

October 16. Weather bad and the wind coming from the east. Looks like heavy weather outside. Shift around to city dock, where a crowd gathers. Newspapermen and photographers want a story. They refuse to give me $5, so I get no story or publicity here.

October 17. Find the wind northwest and the sun shining. I find out how bad the storm really was. The storm was worse in Long Island Sound than in Chesapeake Bay. I hear no man ever lived through a worse storm in a boat the size of the *Queen Mary*. I can hardly believe that I rode through the gale at its height. The life-guards towed many boats in distress. Some yachts were dismasted while in a small cove at Newport News. I must get back to Norfolk again. It is now 3:30 p.m. and I start to get ready, as I am 12 miles up the river. The wind is light, northwest, and I am in for a good sleep.

A storm off Cape Hatteras, North Carolina

October 18. At 6 a.m., the wind is northwest. I steer down the coast some 60 miles toward Hatteras, the much-dreaded cape in the southern waters and the graveyard of many a ship and crew. Set topsail and get down toward Cape Henry. Noon, seas tumbling around in every direction. Sight three steamers. Wind breezing up and hauling ahead. Take in topsail and heave to. The seas are bad. Sight a pilot boat lying off Cape Henry. Haul off to the south. Boat pointing very badly. This is the North Carolina coast, and no harbour for perhaps 300 miles. At 3:30 a.m., the sea is getting smoother. Make a cup of coffee and eat a biscuit with an orange. Togo gets a bone. Tack and haul in on the beach. Tack and stand off again. Heave to and trim down for the night. Sailing distance 30 miles.

October 19. 6 a.m. Light air, northwest. Probably 15 miles off land. Fairly smooth. Try to head reach down the coast. See Cape Henry in the distance. Wind dies out at noon. The boat is drifting northeast in 22 fathoms of water. I'm now out of sight of land. A swell rolls in from the south. At 4:30 p.m., I head up south-southwest. Get a fresh breeze and start sheets. It's getting dark. Steer course till midnight. Flat calm again. Adrift and sailing probably 25 miles. Heave to again. I sleep till 9:30 the next morning.

October 20. Oil calm. Put over my line and catch a couple of small fish. Still no wind. Just a beautiful day. I am approaching Hatteras and the Diamond Shoal lightship. Looks like a northeast gale is coming. I take stock of my food. I have four tins of beans, two tins of tomatoes, one tin of Campbell's bean soup, two tins of corned beef, two tins of clams, two tins of milk, two tins of peaches, two tins of salmon, half a pack of rolled oats, half a pack of flour, half a pack of Lipton's tea, no coffee, half a pound of butter, two loaves of bread, no biscuits, seven potatoes, bacon enough for one breakfast, three eggs, about two pounds of sugar, two apples and three oranges, plenty of salt and pepper, and water. I do not know when I will get to a harbour. A light breeze springs up to the east and a heavy tide northeast. I have sailed probably 120 miles.

October 21. Four days out from Norfolk. Wind breezing north-east. Sea coming from all directions. I feel this northeast gale could last for a week. Is it possible that I am going to be caught near Hatteras? It is getting thick and I am probably some 20 miles northeast from Diamond Shoal lightship. At 12 a.m., seas are very heavy. A large shark has been following me. He is probably 15 feet long. I try to punch him with a pole. I land one in his gills, and he disappears. Looks like a bad night. I hear the faint sound of the fog signal of the Diamond Shoal lightship. I take my bearing from the compass with my flashlight and judge I am half a mile to the leeward of the ship. Haul up southeast and sight lights of the ship lying broadside to the sea. It is blowing heavily. It is now 9:30 p.m. Get up under lee but not too close. They try to throw me a line from the stern of the ship, but I find it too rough. They know this is the *Queen Mary*. I pull out my main mast and lash it fast to the rail. Haul down my foresail and double reef. Blowing badly. Wind northeast. I run the *Queen Mary* off the wind till 4 the next morning.

October 22. I am tired and need sleep. I haul in my foresheet and heave to on the southern board, but before she comes head to wind, a sea smashes over her bow. Realizing how bad the situation is, I put the lifeline from the stern of the boat. My sea anchor is always ready, lashed to the rail. I designed it so that I could cut adrift without leaving the cockpit. Before my little craft can head to, another sea strikes over the beam ends. The third sea smashes in the cabin doors and fills the cabin full of water. Togo swims around in the cabin, crawls up on my bunk, and barks, as the sea smashes over the boat again. I throw over my sea anchor and cut the lashing. This helps to bring her head to wind. She is now almost full of water. I cut my weather rigging and the spar. It falls over on the weather side and this keeps the boat from rolling over. Carrying 500 pounds of ballast, which is tightly floored down, has kept her from sinking many times.

October 23. Morning. The *Queen Mary* is filled with water. I get my large bucket, which I always keep on hand, and bail. I start my long drift to the northeast against the wind and sea. For nearly 60 hours I battle the northeast gales. The canvas that covered my cockpit is split open by the sea that boarded her. It is now 9:30 a.m. I do not expect to live much longer in the face of this terrible sea. I am bailing almost continuously. At 3:30 p.m., it is blowing about 40 miles per hour. The seas are so uneven. The tide runs to windward, so she does not lie well to a drag anchor. I pull out a mattress which is covered with canvas and with my heavy anchor and rope I put out a tide anchor. This helps to keep her head to sea. Night is now coming and the sky is terribly black. It is going to be another bad night. I am very hungry. Everything in my cabin is soaked. It is now 10 p.m. It is very dark and I can hear the heavy seas breaking to windward. I can stop bailing sometimes for 15 minutes or perhaps a half hour till the seas board me again from either side.

October 24. Morning breaks. It looks like a bad morning. I probably made a 10-mile drift during the night. The tide is going to the northeast. With those drag anchors down I probably made 1 mile per hour. At 10 a.m., two bad seas break over the boat in a few minutes. They fill the cockpit half full. I bail out. I tear the bottom board out of the cockpit and remove a little ballast. I get a place to work the bucket through. I have battled many gales in dories on the banks, but I think these are the most dangerous seas I have ever seen. It is noon. I am tired, hungry, and weary, but there's no rest. Again she swings up-beam to the seas. I take two oars and lash them together, making them about 14 feet long. The wash of one I run through the row lock aft. The butt comes up to the cockpit with a strap so it will not wash away. This I use once in a while to help swing her ahead to the heavy sea. But I find myself so tired that I cannot operate it. It is 5 p.m. but no better. I pull open one cabin door and get hold of a small tin of milk. The bread is inedible. It is like a sponge filled with salt water. I find a tin with rolled oats. I mix a few tablespoons in a tin mug with some milk from the tin and try to eat, but another sea smashes over her starboard side and I say goodbye to my rolled oats. At 10 p.m., I think the tide must have slacked a little. She seems to lie more head to, bringing her weight more on the drag anchor. My little goosewing mizzen, which has been riding for the last 36 hours, needs attention. I repair the sheet and haul her flat again. It is now midnight, and the tide again runs to windward. I believe the wind has more force now than it had 12 hours ago. This is my longest spell without bailing, about three hours. I fall asleep and wake up to find myself lying in the bottom of the cockpit. A wall of water breaks over the boat and I am almost afloat on my back. It is now daylight.

October 25. I have more northeast current than I did earlier. I have probably gone 20 miles in the last 10 hours. I am perhaps 55 miles from Hatteras, but still afloat. I hunt for something to eat and find a small tin of Campbell's pea soup. It is the only thing left with a label on it, and it is a great treat under the circumstances. With it I drink a couple of mouthfuls of fresh water. At 11 a.m., the wind seems to be moderating and goes one point east. Boat seems to lie much better and I kneel down in the cockpit and fall asleep. Togo is in the cabin. His barking wakes me up two hours later and I find that the spinnaker sheet has again been carried away. I have some soft copper wire which I use in place of rope and I repair the sheet with it. I then open a tin of dog food and give part of it to my pal. The day wears on. It is now 6 p.m. and the tide is running stronger. This is the first chance I have to bail her dry, and the night looks as though it might be a little better. Everything is wet. I do not have a dry place, but I must again try to sleep and for a couple of hours I do in a kneeling position. I wake up cold and afloat in the cockpit. The night wears on.

Early on in the voyage I fastened a light line to Togo's breast strap so he would not fall overboard. He never went to sleep when I was lying down; he remained on alert. He knew of passing ships and the danger of breakers. When he came and licked my face, I knew he wanted me for something. He would bark and get terribly excited when porpoises dove around the *Queen Mary*. I told him not to do this and after a few times he would just grunt at them. The afterdeck was his hunting ground. Down on the floor by the head of my bunk was his sleeping quarters, and when I was at the tiller or on deck at night, he had a few hours below, or during rainy weather. But when I told him "on deck," he never came down.

October 26. With another terrible squall the wind goes again northeast. The water goes over her from every angle and I am so tired I can hardly bail. I cannot stand this much longer. I sight a large steamer southeast from me. She looks like an oil boat and is heading northeast. The seas are breaking over her clean to the bridge. I don't think I can keep going much longer. It is now noon. The steamer has made probably 6 miles. I can see her clearly now. The wind moderates again. The day wears on. It is now 2:30 p.m. and through the clouds I see the sun, but only for a moment. It looks like it might be better tomorrow—I can only hope. It is 5 p.m. and getting dark. I can probably add another 25 miles on my drift. I try some more rolled oats with milk from the tin, which has probably filled with salt water. I open the door in my cabin. Water is dropping from the ceiling. Blankets, clothes, and everything else are on the floor. The mattress which I used to help keep the boat to the wind has long since chafed off and gone. A bottle with a screw top which I used as a sugar container has washed back into the cockpit, but the sugar is still dry. I eat some rolled oats with a couple of spoonfuls of sugar. It is midnight. Terribly dark. The wind is moderating and going east. The boat is lying almost side to the sea. I haul in my drift anchor, let go of the peak of my mizzen, and hoist it up in full.

October 27. Morning breaks. With a strap around my waist and tied fast to the rail, I come up with the collar around the cut-off part of the spar and pull it out. I step the remaining part of the foremast and tie fast the cut-off lanyards and hoist the reefer sail. With the butt of an oar, I rig out my jib stay and hoist the jib in full. I take a light easterly and steer for Kill Devil Hill station, North Carolina. I run in all day. Wind going more southeast.

Kill Devil Station

October 28. At 3:30 a.m., the stars are shining and I sight the flashes of the Cape Henry light. When I make Kill Devil Hill Station at 4:30 a.m., I see crowds standing on the beach by a dory. They seem to be waiting for me. I am so weak I can't stand. Togo can't even jump from the cockpit. A heavy sea catches me in shoal water and I make a safe landing. Two people are in the water up to their waists and grab the boat. It takes eight men from the life-saving station, along with help from the sea, to haul up the *Queen Mary*. They know who I am from reports they have received. Togo jumps out, runs around in circles, gets his bearings, and runs over the sand almost backwards. I fall out over the side of the boat and am unable to walk without being assisted. I am glad that I made this forced landing, for I could not have survived another night. They take me up to the station and give me some hot coffee. I sleep for 12 hours. In the meantime, they put tackles on my boat and haul her up on the beach.

October 29. I wake up to find a crowd around my boat. Some people are taking small things off the boat for souvenirs. The lifeguards advise me to give up my voyage, saying the *Queen Mary* will never reach Vancouver. The day is fine and the wind light easterly. I look over my little *Queen Mary*. The hull is still intact; the spars were cut off and the rigging carried away. Everything moveable is gone, even the paint has washed off her decks. At noon, I have dinner with the guards. They send messages of my safe landing. I turn in for a good sleep. In the evening a party visits the station and sends a report to the press.

October 30. A fine morning. I start cleaning up the *Queen Mary*. I clean out the cabin and put the sail and everything else on board out in the sun to dry. I can still hardly walk. I am quite comfortable here at this station. The lifeguards are very kind; there's lots to read and plenty of good food.

October 31. I rest all day and meet many people who call to see my boat.

November 1. Gales to the southeast and rain. Breaking off the shoal sand for many miles, it does not seem possible that a few days ago I had come in over that mass of breakers. In the evening, more people come to the station and Togo entertains about 50 of them with his tricks.

November 2. I start to paint the deck. In the afternoon, I repair the sails. The lifeguards are ready to help me and give me anything I need.

November 3. I work all day painting and re-lettering.

November 4. I go into the woods and cut a small pine, which we haul out with a small truck. I work all day turning this stick into a spar. In the evening, Togo gives a concert at the station and entertains about 50 women and children.

November 5. I start in mending the sails. A fine day and I get a lot of work done.

November 6. Get all fittings and supplies. Guards and women bring down many useful things, which I stow carefully on board.

At 5 p.m., I feel the *Queen Mary* is ready for the sea again. But a bad storm blows from the northeast. I will not get away today. I cover the *Queen Mary* with a large sail. At 6 p.m., it is getting dark and raining heavily. The storm will probably last for three days.

November 7. The seas are terribly heavy. By 3 p.m., the wind is moderating and the seas are going down.

November 8. At 9:30 a.m., the guards haul the *Queen Mary* down to the sea. Put out at low tide and head south again. With a light breeze northwest, I sail all day and all night.

A close call

November 9. I have a light northeast breeze which carries me around Hatteras. I anchor in an inlet south of Hatteras, about 50 miles from Beaufort, but not before almost losing my boat. I arrived at 4:30 a.m. It was not yet daylight and I ran on a sandbar. I jumped overboard to shove her aft. I walked forward on the sandbar, but in the meantime her sail caught some wind and she slipped off, leaving me on the bar. I plunged for her stern, which was now in deep water. My hand caught the lifeline and I dragged myself aboard.

November 10. I anchor in what is called Hallens harbour. Some boys come out in a small skiff and I get some bread and fish. I decide to sleep here the rest of the afternoon. According to my plan, I should have been here 22 days ago. It is 5 p.m. when I awake to find a good northwest wind. I get under way and sail till 9:30 p.m. Sail about 20 miles. The sea is very smooth, so I anchor and sleep.

November 11. I get under way. Wind now southwest. I stand off the coast perhaps 20 miles. Expect to get northeast wind but the wind dies out, and I flounce around all night. Sailing distance 20 miles.

November 12. 6:30 a.m. Have a light air to the southward. The wind is breezing up. At 9:30 a.m., I'm probably 10 miles from Cape Lookout. I put out lines and catch a fish. In the evening the winds die out, and I head reach to the south.

November 13. Wind still coming from the south when I arrive in Wilmington. I pick up mail and get supplies. Sail at 5 p.m. Wind very moderate. At 9:30, I anchor under shore and turn in for sleep. About 2:30, I find the wind northeast and get under way and make Cape Fear at about 3:30 p.m. I sail down the coast toward Georgetown. Pick up a good breeze and at about noon find I am very sleepy. The wind goes out to the east and blows up a fresh breeze and shuts down thick. It looks like a bad night. Haul off east-southeast and get off the coast. At about 5:30 p.m., I heave to and get some coffee. The boat is now jogging off to the south and the little cabin gets warm. I fall asleep till about 9 p.m. I wake up to find Togo gone. I do not know at just what time he fell over. The night is very dark, but thankfully I have a good flashlight. I trim my foresheet and tack and zigzag my course back for 20 minutes. With the flashlight I hope to find him. After 30 minutes, I almost give up hope, when I notice a little green speck. He is now within 10 yards of me and a little to leeward. I hear a faint howl, more like a groan. I can't see his black head in the darkness, but I feel sure it is Togo. Slowly I let my boat go ahead to wind and get alongside of my dear pal. I haul him aboard. He is very weak and unable to stand. A part cocker spaniel, he could probably swim for two hours but the strain he was under knowing that he was lost and that I might never find him again left him overwhelmed with fear. I let the boat jog and tend to my pal as best I could. I take him into the warm cabin and by the fire rubbed him down. Then I roll him in my blanket and put him in the bunk. I continue jogging all night and the next morning.

After a while Togo is all right. I am glad I rescued him, for if I had lost my pal I don't think I could have sailed on. He saved my life and the *Queen Mary* so many times.

The Carolina coast

November 14. The wind still on the eastern board. I go in to Georgetown, South Carolina, pick up fresh supplies, and have a good sleep.

November 15. I look the weather over at about 8:30 a.m. and find no chance of moving. It is very calm.

November 16. Still calm.

November 17. I get under way at about 8 a.m. There's a nice breeze. Fair all day. I sail till 9 p.m. I anchor outside of Charleston, South Carolina.

November 18. Nice breeze. Fair all day. Sailing till 9 p.m. Jog along till morning.

November 19. At about 10 a.m., I get to Charleston harbour. Sail up about 4 miles with the wind fair. Tide coming out makes the going rough. It is now a stiff breeze and I sight boats under double reef in company with me. I make harbour, and tie up at the gas station. Many people come to see the *Queen Mary*. We had been reported off the coast. They ask me questions about my voyage. Newspapermen want a story and pictures of the *Queen Mary*. But I tell them, "no pay, no stories." I receive my mail before sailing again.

November 20. Good breeze from the south and I get under way. I sail till 10:30 a.m., when the wind breezes up and it is getting pretty rough. I make Beaufort, South Carolina, at about 10 p.m. A sailing distance of about 60 miles.

November 21. At 9:30 a.m., there's a nice breeze. Fair day. I sail south to Fort Royal Sound and Paris Island. On course and making about 5 miles per hour. At about 4 p.m., I expect to reach Savannah, Georgia. I see high buildings and the lighthouse in the distance.

The Georgia coast

November 22. A lovely morning. I remain in Savannah cleaning up my boat, writing in my log, and sending letters.

November 23. The morning is very fine and the city is quiet. I give a story to the *Savannah Times*. They take pictures of the boat and Togo. I receive some letters from the *Boston Globe* with a clipping of a story that covered my dreadful experience off Hatteras and my gratitude to the crew of the life-saving station who showed me such kindness.

November 24. Wind fair. I sail all day. At noon I have a dinner of fish, which I caught, along with potatoes and boiled onions. Boat jogs in on a sandbar and I remain there for about two hours. It is very smooth. I stay till dark, when the tide rises. I go overboard and shove the *Queen Mary* off, then jog along till morning.

November 25. Made perhaps 35 miles. I sailed till 1 p.m. with a fair wind. Catch some fish then shoot a duck, which Togo brings to me. I am now on the coast somewhere off Brunswick, in southeastern Georgia. I anchor and spend a pretty smooth night.

November 26. I sailed into Brunswick harbour at 10 a.m. I have not been well for two days. It is the first time on my voyage that I complain of my health. I go back to the boat and sleep as much as I can. By land I am about 330 miles from Miami, Florida. My sailing distance down the coast will probably be about twice that.

November 27. At about 8:30 a.m., I get under way. On course again. The afternoon is mild and smooth. At about 8 p.m., I heave to and boil a mackerel. I have sailed about 45 miles.

November 28. At 5 a.m., it is very fine and warm. Calm till noon. The tide carries me about 6 miles. It is getting dark, and still calm. I've probably made about 20 miles.

St. Augustine, Florida

November 29. Light wind. Fair. At noon I make St. Augustine.

November 30. Cloudy and not so warm this morning.

December 1. Many visitors come to see my boat. Some are from Canada. They bring food and dog biscuits. I sell cards and meet friends bound for Miami. Get a good night's rest.

December 2. Wind northeast and tide very high. It has been raining hard for hours.

December 3. A fine morning. Many visitors. Give several little talks on the wharf and sell cards.

December 4. A quiet, somewhat dark and cloudy day. Wind northeast.

December 5. A busy day. Many people come by. Togo gives a performance playing the piano and the drum and high diving. We pick up a little money.

December 6. Wind still northeast.

December 7. I get ready to sail. Togo gives his last performance here on the dock. Sail at 11 a.m. Wind very light but tide fair.

Make about 20 miles and anchor off a sand beach near the canal. I repair my centreboard staff, which has been carried away, and I spend the evening tidying up. Togo jumps overboard and swims ashore. I take a small skiff and pick him up. I have to find him with a flashlight. We were close to the shore, but he could not swim against the tide.

December 8. Good breeze coming from the north. I get under way at 7 a.m. Have a fairly good day's run, about 55 miles.

December 9. Wind still north. It keeps me off course. Sail till noon and have some boiled potatoes and sardines. Light breeze all day. I am now off Indian River. Jib stay carries away. Run forward to fix it and run onto a sandbar. Spinnaker boom falls overboard and drifts away with the tide. Boat works off with the wind. Jib over and run to leeward and get caught on another sandbar. Here I jump overboard and try to pull the boat around against the tide. Togo falls overboard. I wade across the sandbar and pick up him up but lose the spinnaker boom. I solve this problem, but decide to keep off the coast. I sail till dark, when I can see the lights of the city. Pick up fairway buoy and tie up at a pier for night. Sailing distance 55 miles.

December 10. Wind northeast and thick of fog. I've reached the town of Cocoa. Fog lifts at 2:30 and I get a light wind. I make about 5 miles and tie up at a wharf.

December 11. Pick up a light air and get under way at 1 a.m. and drift along with the tide. Sun very hot. Still calm. Clean my boat and shave. No sharks around, so I tie a line on Togo and he has a swim. At 1:30 p.m., I sight a flock of ducks. A light breeze so I sail toward them. I put a couple of shells in the gun. Two fly over me. A nice fat coot does not get by. When Togo brings him aboard, I prepare him for the pot. Wind very light, but tide seems to be going my way. Wind comes south and I stand off the coast. I tack and stand into Palm Bay. It is dark. I probably made about 10 miles.

December 12. A good fresh breeze. I get under way at 5 a.m. Fair wind all day. Make Fort Pearl harbour. Sailing distance 55 miles.

December 13. I sail at 7 a.m. Good breeze and wind from the north. At 10 a.m., the wind dies out. Anchor. Busy all day cooking duck. I am now about 80 miles from Miami. Have a good night.

December 14. Pick up light breeze southeast by east. Have some trouble with centreboard staff, which I later repair. At 10 a.m., get into West Palm Beach and tie up at the city wharf. Many people here from the north. Togo performs on the wharf and picks up some small change.

December 15. Morning dull and wind north. A mix of rain and sunshine all day.

December 16. I've been away from home five months today. At noon I get under way and leave for Miami. I am now in the inside passage. At 10 p.m., tide and wind carry me about 30 miles. Tie up at a wharf on the west side of the narrows.

December 17. Wind very light, make about 10 miles.

December 18. Wind northeast but very light. At 3 p.m., I get a fair tide and pick up a fresh breeze from the north. I see the lights of Miami at 10:30 p.m.

Miami, Florida

December 19. I tie up at an air station at 9:30. Stroll around and get my bearings.

December 20. I go to the post office and find 40 pieces of mail waiting for me.

December 21. At 10:30 a.m., I go to the mayor's office, the Chamber of Commerce, and I get some supplies.

December 22. I start cleaning and painting my boat. The wind is light easterly. Not much sun.

December 23. I finish my painting. I have many visitors and hear much about this warm place where Canadians love to spend their winters.

December 24. Christmas Eve. I sail around to the city dock.

December 25. Christmas morning. The *Queen Mary* is tied up at the Miami City Yacht Basin flying flags and all decorations. Thousands of people pour onto the dock all day and admire my marvellous boat. I meet my old friend Tom Herridge. He said, "Old top, I have a turkey dinner all prepared, but little did I expect to find the old captain and his little ship tied up at this dock."

December 26. Beautiful sunshine. Togo enjoys a run under the palm trees. I get ready for a busy day. After speaking to about 3,000 people over the last two days, I am a bit hoarse. At 7:30, I am glad to pick up Tom and go for a stroll under the coconut trees in a beautiful park.

December 27. A very busy day. Make arrangements to speak on the radio and at a church. Today I sold $11 worth of cards. In the evening I rest quietly on board the *Queen Mary*.

December 28. A fine morning and day. I talk to hundreds of people on the wharf.

December 29. Day fine and lots of business.

December 30. Busy all day.

December 31. Busy day. Making quite a few dollars. Evening spent with Tom at the dog races.

January 1, 1937. A man named Henry T. Johnson of Stratford, Connecticut, gives me my first dime on New Year's Day.

January 2-3. Fine weather.

January 4. In the morning, I haul my boat ashore to raise her cabin so I can sit straight. The cabin had been so low that I have had to sit on the floor with my head bent.

January 5–9. Work on my boat. Weather fine. Many visitors.

January 10. I attend St. Matthew's Church. Have supper with Tom.

January 11–23. I finish work on the boat and sails. Rigging painted and ready for the sea again.

January 24. I launch the *Queen Mary* and sail to pier five, City Yacht Basin.

January 25–27. I remain at the City Yacht Basin pier talking and selling cards. I also speak on the radio.
February 8. I leave the pier and have to pay a dockage fee of $12. This is the first time I have had to pay dockage in any port.

February 9. At 2 p.m., I sail up the river and plan to install a small Palmer 2-horsepower engine. As it is dark, I tie up and have supper. I clean out the boat and fit in the engine bed.

February 10. Northeast and moderate gale blowing. Raining heavily. At 6 p.m., it is still raining, so I clean up and crawl into my little cabin for the night.

February 11. Still raining. My boat is in bad shape. Everything is soaked. I sleep late then clean up and go to the city to get mail.

February 12. A very busy day. I am engaged to give a number of short talks for a Mr. Norman, advertising manager for a chain store. It is now 3:30 p.m. and the rain is still pouring down. At a store I pick up food for myself and Togo. I get a drive back to the *Queen Mary*.

February 13. Still waiting for the engine. In town all day sightseeing.

February 14. I go to church and spend a quiet day.

February 15. Engine arrives, and I spend the next few days installing it.

February 22. With the engine now installed, I start to paint. A rainy spell comes and I do not finish.

February 28. I put the boat in the water. It rains again. I am ready to sail, but I get knocked down by a car in town. My foot and leg are badly bruised, so I have to stay over a few more days.

March 1. I wake up to find I am not hurt badly.

March 2. At 9:30 a.m., the wind is from the northwest and I bid farewell to Miami. I sail till dark, when I make Coolidge Lodge Club inlet, a place known as the fishing grounds of presidents.

Key West, Florida

March 3. Get under way at 7 a.m. Wind fair. Course south-south-west. Sail all day and at 8 p.m. realize I have made 50 miles. Sleep till 3 a.m. I keep on course. Good breeze and a rough sea running.

March 4. I shape my course for Havana. Sail 15 miles. Too much wind and sea direct on beam. Keep off and run for Key West, about 40 miles away. I make port at 5 p.m. I go in and tie up at the pier.

March 5. The steering gear is not working well so I lay the boat on shore and find that a heavy sea had bent the lower rudder gudgeon and rudder step partly off. It will be a few days before I sail for Havana.

March 6. No wind. I take in supplies and food. The mayor visits me.

March 7. I spend the day with the mayor.

March 8. Sail for Havana. After sailing 7 miles I meet a fine breeze from the east. The wind is not in my favour so I run back to the Keys and spend the rest of the day on board a yacht from Portland, Maine.

The Cuban coast

March 9. Light breeze north. I shape course for Havana and sail all day. Wind increases at about 3 p.m. Running all sails. Boat making about 7 miles per hour. At about 7 p.m., I take in the topsail. Sailing distance about 60 miles. I take in mainsail and sail till about midnight under foresail. Trace up jib and heave to. Tide is going east perhaps 2 or 3 miles per hour. Boat will hold position probably till morning. I am perhaps about 120 miles across to Havana. Turn in for a sleep, but am awakened when a sea boards the boat and smashes the cabin. It is 3 a.m., and very dark. Wind now northeast and sea very heavy. There is quite a gale blowing. I stand in the companionway till day breaks. My pump is gone. I have a cold lunch then hoist and set the topsail before swinging off on course.

March 10. Plenty of wind and heavy sea. Making probably 7 miles per hour. At about 10:30 a.m., the wind is howling. At 1 p.m., the visibility is better. By 2:30, it's bright and clear. The sun even breaks out. I see Cuba and Morro Castle, the fortress guarding the entrance to Havana Bay. With the tides changing and my boat drifting, it is hard to find her exact position. In Havana they signal me from the fort. They hoist the British flag and the pilot boat meets me in the harbour and tells me where to anchor. I am visited by customs and pass the requirements of the port. I haul in to the steamship dock to find I am near the customs and post office buildings. When I return from the post office, I find reporters and photographers waiting for me. They drive me to their press rooms. It is now 7:30 p.m. and Togo seems to have enjoyed the day very much.

March 11. Complete the papers needed at the customs.

March 12. I go to the British consul and Lloyd's agent. They will not insure my boat either here or in New York. I'm told my trip looks like suicide.

March 13. Fine day. Wind northwest.

March 14. This is the most beautiful place I have seen on my travels. Togo has a real time here and many pictures are taken of the boat.

March 17. I sail at 1:30 p.m. Wind northwest and the sky does not look so good. My course: southwest by west. I am prepared for a long sail. Have on board more food and water than I have ever carried at one time. I let my boat come to and I catch a couple of small Spanish mackerel. I must not neglect the opportunity to catch fish or birds to add to my supplies during this long sail. I sail till 9:30 p.m. I have probably made 25 miles down the Cuban coast.

March 18. A light breeze all night. This morning it is calm. I start my engine and make a few miles down the coast. But I cannot afford to use gas. I probably make 15 miles. At 10 p.m., I turn in for a sleep.

March 19. At about 7, I pick up a light breeze. On course, southwest by west. I have a feathered hook and I see plenty of mackerel. But the hook seems to be too large. The fish snap, but I miss them. Then suddenly I get one which is just the right size for my dinner. The boat is jibbing back and forth and I get my line snarled up. I throw it over again, partly paid out, when a kingfish about 30 pounds swallows hook, line, and sinker. This is the last I see of him. It would take a clothesline to hold that fellow. It is now 10 a.m. and blowing a gale, so I keep her on course. I sail down the west side of Cuba. The wind starts to moderate. It is still northwest by west. I sight a small island and run in.

March 20. At about 9 a.m., the wind is northeast. I keep off again and run down through the island. The wind is light. At 9:30, I anchor near a small island along with some fishing boats. I boil fish, potatoes, and onions. A good night's rest.

The Mexican coast

March 21. I get going at 6 a.m. The wind is fair. I sail till noon. Wind becomes very light. Drift all afternoon and sight what I think is the island of Cape St. Antonio. At 1:30, I shape my course for Cape Yucatan, Mexico, west-southwest about 130 miles. Sail till 11 with a good breeze northeast. I heave to, as it is getting rough and a strong tide going northwest. Made probably 25 miles. Boat jogs under foresail and I sleep.

March 22. The wind is coming from the east. Set course to southwest and sail on. Have a fairly good breeze. I sail till 1:30 p.m., when I again heave to and head southeast. Boat head reaching under foresail, will probably stem the tide.

March 23. The wind is southeast and very heavy. Course now southwest. I keep off on course but the wind dies out. I sail till dark. At 7:30 p.m., I am worn out and in need of sleep. I anchor and make some coffee. It is now dark, but clear. I get up on my forward deck and sight the light of Cabo Catoche, in the northernmost point on the Yucatan Peninsula. The powerful light is visible for about 20 miles. The wind now hauls southwest, and I decide to have a sleep.

March 24. At about 5:30 a.m., it looks as though we will have a gale from the west. It seems impossible for me to get far as the seas are bad. I jog under the foresail heading south. I have probably sailed 420 miles since leaving Havana. I jog all day and all night. Tide seems to be carrying me to the northeast. No land in sight.

March 25. I'm probably jogging 2 miles per hour. As the foresail keeps pretty well filled, this wind will perhaps last a week. I am now in the Caribbean Sea, and no seaman ever liked this place. The seas are now high and running unevenly and the *Queen Mary* seems to be doing her best to keep them clear of her deck. But on we drive to the south. All night she jogs. The gale is no better. I patiently wait for daylight.

March 26. Will I ever get fair wind again? The sky looks a little different this morning—apparently going more to the south. I tack the *Queen Mary* and head west by north. I judge I am now about 125 miles southeast from the light off Cape Yucatan. She is probably making 4 miles per hour, but labouring heavily, as the seas are rough. Tide seems to be in my favour. It is now about 6 p.m. and I will have to try to get something to eat. Togo looks hungry too. I heave the *Queen Mary* to port, tack, and bring Togo up. I tie a line to his collar. He rolls about for a bit of exercise. There is not a dry stitch on board the boat. I sprinkle gasoline on the burners of my stove and light up. I have been wet for three days, and it is not so warm. Fire does not burn, so I have a cold lunch. Share some corned beef with Togo and keep off again for a night sail at 4:30 p.m.

March 27. From my deck I see the light and know by the flashes it is Cabo Catoche, probably the strongest light on the Mexican coast. I believe that I am still about 20 miles from the light. I sail on till morning.

March 28. I can see both the new and the old lighthouse. I haul around under the western side close to the light and anchor alongside a small skiff. There isn't much paint or anything else left on the *Queen Mary*. I am now quietly anchored, but a moderate gale from the southeast still blows. I am boarded by two men from the lighthouse. One is a customs officer, dressed in a Mexican uniform. He does not speak English. With him is the lighthouse keeper. As this is my first port in Mexico, I have to get my third set of papers. We go ashore at 11 a.m. and start to get the papers ready. They work till 4 p.m. but do not finish. The lighthouse keeper takes me to get a supply of fresh water. I have to wait for the southeast gale to blow itself out before I can sail down the coast.

April 1. By about 6:30 a.m., the wind has moderated. A light wind comes from the north. I have my breakfast, and get under way. At noon I anchor near a little sandy island and find plenty of plover and lesser yellowlegs. I anchor in shoal water near the shore. My dog and my No. 6 shotgun accompany me ashore. In three shots I get 12 of these little birds. I wade back aboard and am sure Togo has enjoyed this sport very much. No chance of getting away from here, so I prepare my birds for a stew. It is 4 p.m. I start my engine and decide to head to some of the islands. Relying on a chart to guide me, I go down about 15 miles and enter a large inland waterway or bay. As it is getting dark, I pull off from the shore and remain there all night. Wind very light. I get out over a coral reef and find the water very shoal. I am probably 2 miles from a small island, which is breaking all around. It is well I did not keep on last night. I pick my way out through the shoal water and get on course again southwest by west and sail 5 miles with a light breeze. When the wind hauls out northeast and blows up a fresh breeze, I set the topsail and sail about 5 miles per hour.

April 2. I take in my topsail as the sea is rough. Wind still northeast and very heavy. I have a cold lunch and sail till about 5 p.m. I see no harbour. It will likely be a bad night. It gets dark and a heavy squall of wind and rain comes from the north. I lower my foresail and I see a large reef of breakers ahead, so I haul off about 2 miles and heave to. Boat heading northeast. I have sailed probably 40 miles.

April 3. I haul in on the coast.

April 4. I sail till noon, when I sight a lighthouse. I haul in close by and hoist my flag. They hoist a Mexican flag and signal me to come ashore. I throw over the lead and find 6 fathoms of water. Throw out my line and catch a large mackerel. The wind dies out calm and I anchor, as the tide is carrying me back. I plan on staying here till morning, so I prepare my mackerel. Sailed probably 35 miles.

Xcalak, Mexico

April 5. I start my engine and drive off shore. Things start to look bad. At daylight I can just see land so I hoist my foresail and shut off the engine; I will try to make Xcalak, down the coast about 100 miles. My food is getting low. The day passes with a heavy sea and plenty of wind. At 4 p.m., I catch sight of a small lighthouse. I am getting close to the coast. I haul by the wind and start my engine. The boat is closed up very tight but the sea is heavy and it looks as though I might get lost. I sight a schooner way off to the south under foresail. I believe she is looking for the channel and Xcalak so I shut off my engine and let the boat jog. The sea is terribly heavy. The schooner runs down close to me and waves me to follow. I do, and we pass through a small channel breaking very heavily on both sides. We anchor in Xcalak.

April 6. At 7 a.m., I get under way to sail for Belize. I sail all day with a fairly good breeze. The night is very dark but the wind is fair, so I continue on. At about 3 a.m., I tie up at the customs dock at Belize and sleep about six hours.

April 7. I clean my boat and do some repairs.

April 8. I spend the day fixing the boat and getting ready to sail.

April 9. I get clearance papers and sail away at about 3 p.m. with a good breeze northeast. Course southeast. By 1 p.m., I have made about 25 miles and haul in by the side of a small island. I drink a cup of coffee and sleep till about 2:30 a.m.

April 10. In the early morning the wind is fair. I sail for Roatán Island, the largest of the Honduras Bay Islands, which is about

120 miles away. At 6 a.m., running along very smoothly. I notch the tiller, make coffee, and heat a tin of soup. The wind is breezing up. She is now making about 6 miles per hour. At 1 p.m., the wind is dead. I set my topsail. I am making fast time across the bay. It is dark and I see a small light. I keep on till midnight and anchor by the side of a small island. I am tired. I have a cup of hot cocoa and turn in for the night.

April 11. Out in the bay the wind breezes up to a moderate gale. I make it to the lee of Cayos Cochinos or Hog Islands. It is about 1:30 p.m. and I run the *Queen Mary* up on the sand. With my dog, I go ashore to stretch out my legs. Though it is blowing a gale outside, I am in a perfect shelter. As I have not a dry stitch on board, I pull everything out and spread it on the beach. When my clothes are dry, I shove off and anchor in shoal water for a good night's sleep.

April 12. The wind has died out and it is now about 6 a.m. I get under way for Trujillo. I have a light breeze from the northwest. The land is very high and was called Honduras by Christopher Columbus, who sailed this coast more than 400 years ago. In 1502, Columbus first saw Honduran soil. He named the area "Honduras," meaning "depths," for the deep water off the coast. At about noon I anchor close to the shore. Nobody comes out, so I put my papers in my cap, jump over, and swim ashore. I find the oldest town in Spanish Honduras. Here I meet the British consul and the governor. I sail across to Castillo and spend the day. A customs officer comes aboard to okay my papers and then another and another. I find this unnecessary. I say "Humbreymarlo papers bro-no. Humbrey bar muse." Another man with him in a small boat hits me on the back of the neck with his fist, so I throw him out of the *Queen Mary*. He climbs aboard his own boat and is paddled ashore. I report the incident to the customs inspector, who has the officer locked up. I weigh anchor and sail around Cape

Castillo. On entering the Caribbean Sea I find a gale coming from the southeast. The sea is very heavy. I run back and anchor in the lee of the cape. It is now 2 p.m. and the wind is blowing a gale. I would not be surprised if I am forced to remain here for several days. I light my oil burner and have a grand dinner of steak, potatoes, and half an apple pie for dessert. Turn in for a good sleep.

April 15. At about 10 a.m., I pull up my anchor and again round the cape. Wind hauls out more easterly. I can lie along the coast by the wind, but both wind and sea are very heavy. The boat is working in on land very fast so I tack and stand off about 3 miles. It's almost impossible to head to the sea. Boat heading now southwest by west. I am starting to move over a sand beach. No harbour tonight. I tack and let my boat reach to eastward. I have sailed about 45 miles.

April 16. It is stark calm and not yet daylight, so I start my engine and steer my course down the coast. Making about 3½ miles an hour. Wind breezes up east again, and I hoist my sails. I see what looks like a cape some 12 miles ahead. I see no name on my world chart, so I anchor by the cape in the lee of a large ledge. I have a big meal and try to write in my log but the boat is rolling too badly. Sailing distance about 45 miles.

April 17. 5 a.m. It is oil calm. I start my engine. Steer along about 15 miles. Wind breezes up and I again get full sail. At noon, close-hauled on course. At 3 p.m., I see a reef of breakers, which I anchor in the lee of, and spend a bad night.

April 18. Light breeze at about 9, so I get under way. Wind breezes up northeast and it gets rough very quickly. Finding I'm in a reef of breakers, I anchor in the lee of this reef and spend the night. Sailed probably 35 miles.

Toward Nicaragua

April 19. A light breeze coming from the east. I start my engine and sail around a horseshoe of breakers till I can get on course. This is False Cape. The tide is strong against me. At 9 a.m., I start my engine and try to get clear of the breakers. I pick up my course again. On my lee bow I see what looks to be a cape. Looks bad. I have not harboured for three nights, so I haul in on the coast to get some shelter. The water is very shoal here and breaking heavy in places. A northeast squall is coming down. The breakers are a long way off this cape. I have to haul in the sheet and start my engine. The going is bad. The boat goes almost completely under. If I do not weather this almighty place, my voyage will end here. I see a fairway buoy and, after more battling, I am able to keep off. What a relief.

On the Nicaragua coast, expecting a squall from the northeast. It's 3:30 and the northeast squall is getting closer. I find myself against the weather shore of this dangerous cape. I haul in my sheet, start my engine, and try to get around this dreaded spot. The wind hauls out east. Seas are terrific. Time and again the *Queen Mary* goes almost completely under. The hatches are on the cockpit. I steer from the companionway. Get around this cape or be lost, I say to myself. It's only about 3 miles and I see what looks like a red buoy marking the starboard shoal water. I feel good when I ease off the sheet around this dreaded cape. I anchor in shoal water in the bay where 400 years ago Columbus anchored also seeking shelter. "Thanks be to God," I repeat to myself. The squall passes over, and I lie quietly anchored.

April 21. I am on the line between Honduras and Nicaragua. I get under way, with the wind northeast, and sail down the coast for the port of Bluefields. Expect to report and get supplies. For breakfast I have 12-day-old bread. It is all the food I have. I make Bluefields harbour at about 6 p.m. I anchor and spend the night.

April 22. Report to customs. I meet the mayor and the police captain. They arrange for my meals at a restaurant for as long as I stay. I clean up and have supper.

April 23. A quiet day. I am very tired, having had little sleep since I left Trujillo. Over the next few days, I believe half the people in town come to see the *Queen Mary*. Many of them speak English. I am invited to have supper with a sea captain and to give a talk to some 300 people at the dock.

April 24. Wash up boat and take in supplies.

April 25. The locals wake me up as they all want cards or pictures. I can't sell any more as their money is no good to me when I leave here.

Costa Rica

April 26. I get ready to sail. I have $19 of local money, which I spend on clothes and a flashlight. I leave the rest of my change there. I clear for La Union, Costa Rica. It is now 10 a.m. Wind northeast and fair. I sail down the coast. At about 9 p.m., I see the new moon. I heave to and let the boat jog to the south.

April 27. I have some coffee and keep off on course at 5 a.m. The wind is still east. Sail till noon. No land in sight and, at 7:30, I heave to again. Eat soup, tea, and bread and jam. Keep off on course and expect to see land. Sailed perhaps 35 miles. Sight land but it is getting dark. It is probably the city of Limon. Wind fair. I sail all night. A good breeze. Should be down to Costa Rica by early morning.

April 28. Reach Costa Rica at about 9:30 a.m. and haul into the customs wharf. Ship's papers are examined. Dinner at a hotel and afternoon spent sightseeing.

April 29. It is a fine day and I make some repairs on the sails. I re-rig everything. Will probably be here for a few days. I have to get my supplies from government agents.

Heading to the Panama Canal

April 30. I rest all day. Many people come down to see the boat. I get my supplies and sail at about 2:30 p.m. for the canal. Wind fair, a nice breeze coming from the northwest. I sail till dark. Let boat jog and make some supper. Wind hauls out northeast and shuts down, thick of fog. It's not good, but I keep going all night.

May 1. Still thick of fog and wind fair. Probably sailed 100 miles or about halfway across the Mosquito Gulf to Panama. Fair wind and fog stays all day. Heave to and have supper. Let boat jog south till morning. Boat lies pretty quiet there. Not much tide. All is calm. No drifts or sounds. I turn in to sleep till 4:30. Have breakfast. Start the engine.

May 2. I am steering east. Light breeze springs up. Getting along perhaps 4 miles per hour. I sail all day and all night. Nice breeze. I am now 50 miles from the canal. I heave to and sleep for about five hours.

May 3. I start the engine and sail till noon. It is still thick with fog. I stop the engine and listen. I pick up the blast of a steam ship. Take bearings of the sound and haul in for the canal. Run in south for one hour. Fog lights up here and I am almost directly in the entrance. I run in and anchor off the customs docks. I go to the cable office and they send a wire home saying that the *Queen Mary* has safely arrived in Panama.

May 4. I am now in the colonial city of Cristobal at the gateway of Limon Bay. I am about halfway on my voyage. I visit the port city of Colon and the dock from where I once sailed. I loaded freight there 40 years ago while employed by the Panama and Pacific Steamship Company. The customs and harbourmaster come aboard my boat and arrange to have me enter the locks in the morning.

Through the Panama Canal

May 5. A pilot comes aboard at 9 a.m., and I enter the locks. We rise about 27 feet in seven minutes. We enter the second lock, and rise again. Through the third lock, the rise brings us to the same level as a freshwater lake. Locks at each end to lift ships up to Gatun Lake, an artificial body of water created to reduce the amount of excavation work required for the canal. It is 85 feet above sea level. The freshwater lake was a great valley before it was flooded. A low, muddy, slimy swamp, it was almost impossible for anyone to walk there. It was home to the mosquito that from its sting dealt out death to the labourers attempting to build the canal. Within 3 miles of the Pacific there are three more locks which let boats down to the level of the Pacific Ocean.

The water of Gatun Lake is perfectly fresh. I make a cup of tea with it and both Togo and I have a swim. It is the first fresh water I have been in for nine months. Under power of my engine, it takes about nine hours to get from the Atlantic to the Pacific. I anchor in the town of Balboa and tie up at the wharf for the night. Visitors come to see my boat and wonder how such a small speck made it through the canal.

Into the Pacific

May 6. I go ashore and meet canal officials. They give me a card of welcome from the Balboa Yacht Club. A pilot accompanies me around. They make arrangements for my food and for my boat to be hauled out and painted. I feel very welcome. They also arrange for Togo to give a performance in the ballroom.

May 7. I spend the day sightseeing and the afternoon getting ready to sail.

May 8. Many visitors.

May 9. Dinner at the club and spend the day with friends visiting the hospital.

May 10. At about 5 a.m., with a light air coming from the east, I sail into the Pacific for my long trip up to Vancouver. I set course to Cape Mala, Panama. A good breeze springs up and I run off till 1:30 p.m., when I make tea and have lunch. I have averaged perhaps 5 miles an hour. At 4:30 p.m., the wind is getting light and hauling east. Not long after, I sight land off to starboard. It is now dark. I am probably 30 miles from Cape Mala. Heave to. At 10 p.m., I turn in, and sleep till morning. At 5 a.m., a heavy thunder and lightning squall calls me on deck. My first night on the Pacific.

May 11. Wind light east. Seeing light some 10 miles away, I steer for Cape Mala. The wind dies out and I start my engine. Steer across to Point Mariato, a cape which is at the southernmost point on the mainland of North America. I round at 3 p.m. and sail till dark. A stiff breeze coming from the west. My sailing for the day ends. I heave to and the boat ranges off southwest. I have probably sailed 180 miles since leaving the canal.

May 12. Can see land, so keep the engine running all day. It is now dark. I have to turn off at Coiba Island, the largest island in Central America. There's thunder, lightning, and a gale of wind. Put over drag anchor and boat washes with seas all night. Glad when morning breaks. I am still afloat, but somewhat of a wreck. How this little boat survived the last nine months amazes me.

May 13. At 6 a.m., the skies are very heavy. Wind light northwest. Tide now running southeast. I am probably 30 miles off the coast. Haul up northwest by west. It is very rough. At 11 a.m., I start the engine but find thunder and lightning has cut off wires, so I have to heave to and do some repairs. I will try to get under land for this looks like another bad night. But wind comes off the north as I am approaching the coast of Costa Rica. I will not likely get into port. I keep canvas over the boat and finish my repairs. I try to make a fire and get some coffee. Everything is wet on board, so I have a cold lunch. There is nothing more I can do, so I cover my cockpit and turn in. The seas pound the *Queen Mary* till 4 a.m. Not much sailing distance today, perhaps 20 miles.

May 14. The wind hauls around again northwest. I stand in on the land and find I am about 15 miles east of the Costa Rican border. I haul in a small place where I see a dock and some warehouses. I tie up and mail a few letters. At 1 p.m., I am ready to sail. This place is Barid Bay. The wind is northeast. I have a fairly good run, round Cape Mala, and heave to at 9:30 for a meal and sleep.

May 15. Light breeze northeast. I start the engine and get well up across Coronado Bay. At 3 p.m., the wind dies out. It looks like a nor'wester is coming. I haul by the wind and cross the Gulf of Nicoya, an inlet of the Pacific Ocean in Costa Rica. Here the wind comes off the northwest. There's a stiff breeze, and it gets rough. It is 9 p.m. and too rough to sail the *Queen Mary*. I heave to, heading south. Tide going northeast. Going offshore very fast. Cover everything and turn in. Seas smashing over the boat. At midnight thunder and lightning fill the sky. Wind rounds the compass, back and forth. It seems impossible we will live till morning. Sail down. Everything lashed. Mizzen reefed and sheeted flat. Sea anchor over but boat does not lie head to wind. Lightning strikes and blows out the generator. Blows mizzen and after-hatch off. Another flash strikes down through the centreboard box. Seems to have followed the steel centreboard down and comes out the side of the boat. She rolls over. Water coming in her cockpit. Another flash strikes starboard on the water tank, but does not damage the hull. Wind draws in more north. This is too bad! I am a wreck, but hope for daylight to come soon. Tide and wind are carrying me a long way off the coast.

Tough going off Cape Blanco

May 16. Morning. The skies are black and wind northeast. Too rough to sail, so I haul in drag anchor and hoist reef foresail and head northwest by west. I am making a broad drift. Noon, seas are heavier, wind draws more northeast. I try to make coffee, but find water tank dry. I realize I have no water. The lightning made a small hole in the tank. I have a gallon jug for drinking water only, but it half is full. The wind hauls more northeast and I am forced to make land. My engine is out of commission from the storm. I have no choice. I have to land wherever I can. I have been drifting and pounding around for the last 24 hours. I'm probably 70 miles southwest by west from Cape Blanco. I put up my mizzen and stand her in place again. I make the *Queen Mary* work for the next 36 hours as I try to get to land. At 6 p.m., darkness comes on and I steer from my companionway. My head is covered part of the time with a canvas hood under reefed mizzen foresail and jib. *Queen Mary* pounds northwest by west.

May 17. Weather no better, but wind inclined to go northeast. Boat heads up northwest. Seems to moderate a little, so I put two cups of water in my kettle and, with a rag soaked in oil, I get my stove dried out. While the boat pounds on toward land, I get some coffee made—the first in three days. Everything is wet. I open a tin of corned beef and with some mouldy bread make a meal. I share the meat with Togo, who looks at me with his soft eyes as if to say, "Not so good, Bill." He drinks a little cold coffee, and the lunch seems to give the situation new life. I slip on my bridle again, which is just a short strap that lets me move around the boat so that if I am washed overboard I can pull myself back again. This rope has saved me several times already. I shake out the reef from the foresail and am able to give her a pretty good fill. It is 4 p.m. but still no sight of land. I am making better time. The seas perhaps are a little smoother. At about 10:30 p.m., I see a few stars. Clouds travelling out from the northeast. Should make land tomorrow. I am terribly worn out and sleepy. I am perhaps making 3 miles per hour. Tide seems to have slacked a little, so I let the *Queen Mary* take care of herself for the next few hours. At 3 a.m., I find the boat heading north. Better. Have a cold lunch and take the tiller. She makes north and is probably travelling 4 miles per hour.

Washed overboard

May 18. Morning. I sight land and believe it to be the coast of Nicaragua. Boat does not head up so well. Wind seems to draw back northeast. At noon, I try to find lunch of some kind. Sun is shining bright and warm. Togo goes and smells the jug, so I know he wants water. I have a tin of tomatoes, and crackers, very damp. Give him a small drink of water. I am now within 5 miles of the coast. But it will be impossible for me to land on account of the heavy sea. At 5 p.m., I am within half a mile of the most deserted-looking place I have ever seen. It is not safe for me to sail any longer. At 7 p.m., I anchor in 8 fathoms of water.

May 19. I use two more cups of water and have coffee with the last of my bread fried in some fat and syrup and fried eggs. Togo has some dog food, which he eats readily. I now get under way and sail up the coast, trying to find a place to land. The seas against these sands and cliffs are terrible. At 10 a.m., I see a few shacks but not a soul or a safe place to land. The tide seems to be running westerly close to the shore and pushing me very fast with it. I need water. I see a few small buildings and a couple of men working on one. They look as though they are clearing a small farm. Water is very shoal here and breaking a quarter of mile off the coast. They see me, but I sail on, trying to find a place to land. I am probably 100 miles east of Corinto, Nicaragua. I see two large cliffs with an opening of some 50 yards between them. It does not seem to be breaking across this place. By making a couple of short tacks, I get in near the breakers. I find there is a little sandy spot inside of the western cliff, but nobody for miles around. I haul the *Queen Mary* close to the western cliff and she loses her headway. I have her completely covered up and battened tight, and the first roller lifts her up. Having no headway to start with, she stops near the end of the west cliff. I grab an oar and get on my cabin. With my left arm in the rigging, I try to shove her bow off from the cliff. Just as I am feeling sure that my voyage will end here, another sea breaks from the end of the eastern cliff, runs across and picks up the *Queen Mary* and lands on top of the western cliff. I am pushed out the starboard side and into the Pacific.

I still hang on to the butt of the broken oar as I come to the surface and crawl aboard as she rolls down. I must still try to save her. I untie my spinnaker boom and am again ready for the next sea. Togo is already on land. Standing on the sand, he barks excitedly at me. The water is very deep between these two cliffs. I look around and another heavy sea picks up the boat and rolls her over on her beam ends. With the end of a small line that I have tied fast to her stern head for this purpose, I plunge into the waters of the Pacific, attempting to swim ashore. As she has a hole in her hull below the waterline and is filling with water, she can't seem to get clear of the vortex. I am clad in nothing more than a pair of cut-off pants. The sea tosses me around and I try to shake off the rope, which has become tangled around my left leg. I find bottom with my feet and with my head above the surface I haul the *Queen Mary* onto the sand. She lands on her starboard side in as bad a condition as I expected. I can see a small hole in her port side below the waterline. I take my anchor and run up the beach and throw it among the roots of a large tree.

As the Pacific rolls her up on the sand beach, the tide turns and starts to fall. I made a lucky landing. The sands are fast burying her. Over half of her is buried to the washboard. It is now 4 p.m. and, to make matters worse, it is raining. I rig up the sail and try to catch some rain water, but the squall prevents it from amounting to anything. One of my cabin doors has been broken. The boat is lying on her starboard side half full of water. Of all my troubles since leaving Nova Scotia on July 16, this seems to be the worst. I start clearing out my cabin. I carry my little oil stove up to the beach and, after some time, I get it lit. My matches were kept in a glass bottle that I got at the canal. I finish the last of my fresh water. I go up on the sand above the high-water mark, and find tracks. I follow these for about 2 or 3 miles till I reach a wagon road. I find a small shack and a man who says "Hombre agua." He gives me two coconut shells full of water and follows me down to my boat. He invites me to sleep at his hut with him, but I do not want to leave the *Queen Mary*. I sleep under my wet blanket.

May 20. The kind man comes back early in the morning. After much trouble getting him to understand what I need, he says "Le Ambra," which I find to be a small town 40 miles from the start of this road. He signs hat he will be back at 2 p.m. tomorrow. I show him the part of the engine that has been disabled by the thunderstorm and write on a card what I want. I give him an American $10 bill, and he leaves. Now I start clearing up the boat. With the sun shining, today I will get dried. I have repair tools and lumber that I brought. I work and then have some tea, cook a mackerel, and boil some rice which the locals brought me. Togo eats dog food because there is nothing else. He has never liked dog food.

May 21. The day is fine. I repair the sails and patiently wait for the man to return. Five people make an appearance at about 3:30. They have a couple of tins of water, some food, two tins of gasoline, and small fittings for my boat. I place the fittings in my engine and gather my belongings. By dragging down some drift logs and roots, I build an abutment on the port side of the boat. The tide will be high at midnight, when I had planned on floating the *Queen Mary*. With the blade from my broken oar I start shovelling sand from under the boat. At 12, the first sea lifts her bow and, with the help of another roller, I shove the *Queen Mary* off. The night is fine, but there's a heavy sea running. My engine turns over with the first click. A few minutes before launching, I cut the line I had running from the port bow to the root of a tree and hurriedly throw it across the bow. The seas which boarded her on the bow caught the rope and wrapped it around the propeller blade. The boat stopped right against the ledge which had broken her side during our landing. Without a thought I caught the lifeline aft and jumped overboard. I grabbed the rope that hung from the propeller and came to the surface. To my astonishment, the engine turned off as easily as it had turned on. In a few seconds the *Queen Mary* was heading to sea again under power. I could have been a wreck on that cliff. I thank God this is over and once again shape my course for Corinto, some 40 miles away.

May 22. The morning is fine with a light wind coming from the east. I shut off my engine and hoist the sails. Let the boat sail along while I make badly needed breakfast. Have a fairly good breeze all day. At about 9:30, I heave the *Queen Mary* to and have more eats and a wink of sleep.

May 23. I should make Corinto by night. The wind now northeast. The *Queen Mary* is under full sail near the coast. The sea is fairly smooth, and she is doing her best. At 5 p.m., I am at the entrance of Corinto harbour, a small port on the Nicaragua coast. A customs boat loaded with soldiers meets me and shows me where to anchor. The British vice consul asks me to come to his office in the morning.

May 24. The captain of a British ship gives me a case of gas, food supplies, and a new lantern. I have dinner on board at his table. The British consul tells me he was born in Nicaragua and became vice consul after the death of his father. I finally get my papers at 4:30 p.m. By 5 p.m., I hoist the sail on the *Queen Mary*. I am anxious to keep going. I make some 15 miles up the coast with a northerly wind, when the wind jumps around to the northwest and I run into one of the worst storms I have ever experienced. At 9 p.m., I haul down my sails and cut away my drag anchor. Thunder and lightning rend the sky and the boat is going back to the southeast with the tide and wind. I put the hatches on my cockpit and cover it with canvas. I can't remember ever seeing it darker. The sea runs from every angle. Rain falls in squalls and lasts about two hours.

May 25. I hoist the reefed foresail and haul in the sea anchor, so she pounds down the sea jogging slowly southwest. The storm lasts all day. Wind and rain. I go into this night again with the sea anchor down all night and all the next day.

May 26. The stars come out. The last squall seems to have blown itself out. Everything in the boat is wet. Little sleep and little to eat. I am so tired I can hardly stand. I lie down on the cabin floor. Togo, too, has felt the effects of this long siege. He cuddles with me and keeps me warm. When I wake up, the sun is shining and the sea is smoother. With a gasoline-soaked rag I start the stove and make some coffee. My spirits are raised and I get under way. The weatherman seems to have poured out the last of his northerners and we now have a light air to the southeast. My position at this time is about 40 miles southeast of Corinto. My worry now is how I am going to run clear of these squalls over the last two days. Light air springs up into a moderate breeze. By 7:30 p.m., I have sailed backwards some 30 miles. The night is fine. The stars are out and I have every hope of running through these easterly squalls. All night I steer the *Queen Mary* northwest by west.

May 27. My lost distance has been recovered. I prepare food and get a few winks of sleep. Togo's barking wakes me. He is after his old enemies again, the porpoises, which seem to be doing everything but jumping aboard the boat.

May 28. I sail all day on course. Will make the coast of El Salvador. Getting up toward La Union Bay, an inlet of the Gulf of Fonseca. It is a bay always ready to blow a small boat out of the water. Wind still hangs light southeast. I have every hope of making a few hundred miles without more bad thunderstorms. At 6:30 p.m., I am up in what I consider the mouth of La Union Bay. Wind still fair. Sight coast of El Salvador and a small steamer coming out of the bay. Sail till 10 p.m. and let the *Queen Mary* jog while I get food.

Along El Salvador

May 29. At about 4:30 a.m., light air northwest. Run up the coast all day. Have been by the wind all day. Tide running southeast. Can see land. Fine day. Speak to steamer *Indea* and he slows down for my signal. This is a large Swedish motor ship bound for Vancouver. I go aboard and get water and supplies. At dark I shove off and they move out of sight. Weather now calm. I start the engine and head up northwest by west again. Do not make much headway as strong tide coming southeast. I run till midnight.

May 30. I have sailed some 300 miles since I left Corinto. No wind. Boat drifts southeast probably 10 miles. Calm all day.

Toward Puerto San José

May 31. Have a light northeast breeze and will head up the coast for Puerto San José, Guatemala. Wind breezes up northeast.

Might have a good run. By noon the wind dies out. Boat going southeast again. Clouds coming up to the west. At 7 p.m., thunder and lightning. Have foresail and jib down and furled. Throw over sea anchor. This looks like another bad night. Maybe blowing 50 miles an hour.

June 1. Calm again and sun shining. Start engine, but not much gasoline left. Find gas line choked up with water in cylinders from heavy roll. Start repairs. Have dinner. Start engine again and will try to make San José. Wind again northeast. Going looks better.

June 2. I again drift southeast probably 8 miles. Get wind northeast and I haul in northwest. At noon I sight land. By about 5:30 p.m., I am on the coast again. Throw over the anchor and find I have 20 fathoms of water. Will spend night here.

June 3. Calm. Boat tailing southeast so lie to anchor and catch some fish. I do not know what they are, but they make good eating just the same.

June 4. I have about three gallons of gas, so I decide to get moving. I am probably 50 miles from San José. It is now 9 a.m. and I run my engine till about 2 p.m. I anchor in about 22 fathoms of water.

June 5. Awakened by a squall from the north, which I take advantage of anchored off the coast of San José. It is too rough to get near the dock but they send a surf boat out and I send ashore my papers and $10. They send me out two cases of gas, five gallons of water, bread, other supplies, and 85 cents change. I stop here two hours and then start sailing up the coast. It looks as though it might be a good run. I am now approaching the Gulf of Tehuantepec, in southern Mexico. "Look for squalls in this bay," I am told. I keep on till dark and, as I am close on the coast, I anchor. Have boiled mackerel and potatoes before I sleep.

Salina Cruz, Mexico

June 6. Find the wind southeast. I get under way and set topsail. I go into Salina Cruz and find the harbour closed. This was a great shipping port before the Panama Canal officially opened in 1914. Steamers loaded at Seattle, Vancouver, and San Francisco and unloaded at Salina Cruz. Freight of all descriptions was shipped through to the Atlantic port by rail. A large amount of English capital was spent at Salina Cruz to build docking facilities. This, of course, saved ships from making the long trip around the Horn. When the canal was finished, ships no longer unloaded their cargos at this port. Salina Cruz was forgotten and banks of sand closed up the entrance of the harbour. On my arrival there was not even a trace of water running in or out of this harbour. I get as close as I can to the shore and, with my papers in my cap, I go ashore and meet customs officials on the breakwater. I tell them I landed to pick up mail, but they keep me all day and want me to get an agent. They say I must get papers, for which they want 15 pesos. So Togo and I put in one of the hottest days I have spent on earth. At 4:30 p.m., I go to customs again. It looks as though I will not get my papers this day. I have stuff to take aboard my boat but cannot get anyone to take me out.

In a pub next to customs are some fellows who speak both Spanish and English. I have a brain wave and decide to go *loco* (crazy). I do this by rushing about, shouting at the top of my voice. I throw my cap at the customs officer and make believe I am going to hit him. He rushes out into the street and cries, "Capitaino loco!" They gather around me saying, "Poor Capitaino." In a few minutes they get my papers, give me some food and gas, and four men launch a boat from the sand and row me out to the *Queen Mary*. Now I am not so crazy. I get under way. It is dark when I start my engine, head up the coast, and heave to till daylight.

Toward Acapulco, Mexico

June 7. The land along this coast is filled with high sandhills and cliffs. There are plenty of fish too. The morning is calm, so I catch a couple. Will try to get into Acapulco some 300 miles up the coast. The wind comes off the northwest, making the going very bad. Tide and wind ahead, so I go offshore very quickly and up comes another thunderstorm. It gets very rough. Boat under foresail all night.

June 8. I am out of sight of land. It is very rough. I have probably made 40 miles.

June 9. Still going offshore. No use to tack so I keep on reaching southward.

June 10. I must be 100 miles off the coast. Sight a steamer. Wind hauls northeast. I set topsail and at 10:30 wind gone out east. I haul in for land again northwest but wind goes right around the compass and seems to stand at northeast. I haul down the topsail; heading northwest again. Boat sails along and I prepare some supper. Boil a fish and have tea and some of my Salina Cruz bread. Jog under foresail and turn in for sleep. Midnight, look out and see black clouds and lightning. Jog along at probably 2 miles per hour.

June 11. I had a bad dream, which might mean trouble. At 4:30 a.m., I again steer her along. Wind moderates and I start the engine, but something goes wrong with my magneto. I take it apart, but find I cannot repair it. Boat is heading northwest by west, so I sail all day. Will try to get in to Acapulco. Wind comes northeast, and I set topsail. I sight land again. I hope this wind keeps up. Engine not working. I steer the boat all night on course.

Resting at Acapulco

June 12. At about 4 a.m., I see light. Wind has gone out east again. I think this is Acapulco. At about 5:30 a.m., I get into the mouth of the harbour. The wind dies out, and I anchor. Motor launch comes along, tows me in, and charges me 8 pesos.

June 13. I haul my boat out. She is leaking badly; the worms have eaten through. Find a man who speaks good English. He arranges to have my boat hauled out. We haul her up on the beach and some people from Mexico City visit. This is a large, egg-shaped bay probably 10 miles in length and 5 miles wide. At the entrance is a nice harbour. The city lies west of this and is noted as a place of shelter. The whaling fleets and sailing ships that used to round the Horn came here when they needed repairs. Here I get the *Queen Mary* cleaned and repaired. I pick up a few pesos from the people who buy cards from me.

June 14. I launch off again. Josh H. Woods gives me three gallons of gas and Mr. and Mrs. Beebe fit me out with bread and supplies.

Manzanillo, Mexico

June 15. I sail from Acapulco for Manzanillo. The wind is east and fair. I sail till 9 p.m., when I make anchor near the coast. Made 35 miles.

June 16. Wind west. No course. Get under way early. Head work all day. Distance sailed 35 miles, gained about 10 miles.

June 17. A stiff breeze southeast. Weather bad, and getting rough. At 10 a.m., I am under foresail. Have double-reef foresail. Wind blowing about 50 miles per hour. Now have only a jib. I am near the coast, and I see what looks like a cape. I might find shelter. See high cliffs and a lighthouse. I haul in toward the end of the cape, but the sea is very heavy. The boat is battened down and I steer from the companionway. I keep as near to the end of the cape as possible; I jib this double-reef foresail and it nearly takes the spar out. I round a high cliff and shoot into smooth water. As

I look out on the angry Pacific, I wonder how the *Queen Mary* lived through those high seas. I start my engine and go up in a small bay and let go of both anchors. I am directly between two mountains. Water is as smooth as a mill pond. But the wind blows through this valley and, for a while, she drags those two anchors. Sailing distance about 80 miles.

June 18. A fine morning. Sea heavy, so I start my Palmer. As it is calm all day, I run perhaps 30 miles. In this run I see many kinds of fish. Some are probably 500 pounds. I believe they belong to the skate family. I catch some small fish. After boiling them, I enjoy eating them. Dark. Stop engine. Probably drift 5 miles southeast.

June 19. Light air northeast. Start my engine. At 1:30 p.m., make Manzanillo. Pass necessary port requirements.

June 20. This harbour has a breakwater running westward that prevents a southerly roll and winds from the Pacific. A few steamers call here with mail and freight. The people in this little town seem very free and easy. Surrounded by high land, it is very hot, and the water system is poor.

June 21. I go to the customs house. Nobody speaks English. Everybody seems to have my papers but the right man. I go to Graceline Steamship office and find a Mr. Robert Burett. He straightens things out for the *Queen Mary*. I buy gas and supplies. I am satisfied when I again point the *Queen Mary* up the coast.
June 22. Calm all day till midnight, when there is a wind and thunderstorm.

June 23. She goes along by the wind while I make coffee. I probably made 25 miles. Fine. Wind north. The tide is in my favour. Sailing slowly to the west. I start my engine and, at about 10 p.m., I let the *Queen Mary* head reach while I sleep.

June 24. No wind. Plenty of fish around. Light wind to the west so I stand *Queen Mary* on the coast. I start my engine and run in around some high cliffs. Find Togo has ticks on his neck. I have sailed about 25 miles. I will not get out of this tomorrow, as the wind will be westerly. I tend to Togo's ticks and repair the sails.

June 25. I remain here and do my repairs. In the evening the wind goes southwest. I get under way at about 4 p.m., make about 20 miles, and heave to.

Mazatlán, Mexico

June 26. I get a fresh squall from the east and the *Queen Mary* runs off the wind with all sail. At about 7 p.m., I arrive in Mazatlan to find I have been reported by the Graceline manager at Manzanillo. I meet the manager, and he has my papers fixed up.

June 27. I stay quietly at the pier.

June 28. Go to customs, post office, and the British consul and find there will be no gas here for perhaps a week. I have dinner and see the city. I learn that the city was named "place of deer" by the Indians because the animals were so plentiful.

June 29. Meet a teacher named Mrs. Watson and have dinner with friends.

June 30. My papers are ready. I meet the first man said to have sent relief to Halifax from Mexico after the Halifax Explosion in 1917. The explosion occurred when the SS *Mont Blanc*, a French cargo ship loaded with wartime explosives, collided with the Norwegian vessel SS *IMO* in Halifax harbour. Mr. Lyle is 76 years old. He gives me a case of gas and some food. The British consul and his wife visit my boat.

July 1. Meet Max Germain from the brewery. He gives me a peso and five gallons of gas. He repairs my water tank and puts a new primary cup on my engine. Have a visit from the American consul, and a Mexican writer comes aboard. He gives me $2 for a story. Mrs. Watson, the teacher, brings down some schoolchildren. They sing four songs in English for me. This makes me homesick, so I dip my flag and sail for Cabo San Lucas, at the southern tip of the Baja California Peninsula. Sail till dark and make about 30 miles.

Off to California

July 2. Wind southeast. I get under way at 4 a.m. Sail southwest till about 10 p.m. It is quite a gale. It is terribly rough. Have made about 60 miles.

July 3. Still a good breeze. Get under way at 6 a.m. I have been wet for two days, and my eyes are so bloodshot I can hardly see. I have had a continuous spray of salt. The tide runs southeast against the wind and it is very rough. It is now thick of fog but I must have cleared off another 60 miles. I have some doubts about my position just now, so I let the boat head reach under the foresail.

July 4. Get under way at about 4 a.m., and sight land. I get in under the cape in a sheltered place at about 3 p.m. and find that the sun is shining. Start a fire, and have dinner. Dry things. The wind moderates and here I get my first good night's sleep in a week.

July 5. Get under way at 4 a.m. but find the wind ahead. At 9 a.m., I am heading northeast by east and slowly drawing out in the Pacific again. The tide is carrying me fast to the east, out of sight of land. I tack, and the boat heads along on the western board again. As the wind heads me off, I stand in toward Cape San Lucas. Wind west-southwest and, at 10 p.m., I sight lights 10 miles east of Cape San Lucas. In a small cove I anchor. As food and water are none too plentiful on board the *Queen Mary*, I row over alongside a yacht and find they are only too willing to give me anything I need to help me along on my voyage.

The long drift

July 6. After giving me food, supplies, and a can of gas, the people on the yacht take pictures of the *Queen Mary*. I get under way at 10 a.m. and head along up the cape. Wind strong, so I haul into the shelter of a cape, and anchor. It is too rough to keep on. I am now under the eastern end of California. At about 6:30 p.m., I get under way, stand off about 3 miles, when I get a stiff nor'wester and thunder. Another bad night.

July 7. At 4 a.m., I find the wind has gone out southwest, and I go back on course again. At 9 a.m., I sight what looks to be a fishing boat under sail coming down the coast. A good breeze till dark, and make around 50 miles. Many seals around me all day. Wind heads me off. I get on the coast again and travel along a sand beach perhaps 100 miles more. Seas seem to be heavy and running far on the sand. I find 8 fathoms of water, anchor, and stay here till morning.

July 8. Get under way at 5 with a light breeze to the north. I sight land to the north, but wind hauling fast to the northwest heads me off. Noon, I have some food. It looks like a bad night and that I might get far off my course in the bay.

July 9. I head up toward Cedros Island. Made probably 25 miles. I sight a large steamer. They pass this cape very close. Course northwest, 200 miles to Cape Pablo. I have little gas, so will likely be blown away in the bay, probably 50 miles off course. The wind blows sometimes for weeks here. I anchor in the bay, making 35 miles.

July 10. Light northwest wind, so I run my engine till 10 a.m. I head reach under foresail. Sail all night.

July 11. Wind light. Wind moderates at 9:30. Sight small boat, so I tack and stand in the bay. I am far off my course. Meet some Mexican fishermen. They do not speak English. They cannot even tell me the name of the place they are fishing from. I pick up four more fishermen and I tow them into a small cove. They do not speak English but can say "gasoline," so I anchor the boat and go ashore. Have dinner in their shack. No bread. They are 30 miles from any town and flour is too expensive for them to buy. Their shack is the hardest looking place I ever saw. The weather is warm. They walk about 3 miles for water, which they get from a mud hole. Their boat is a long dugout, a frail looking craft and terribly patched up, probably about 30 years old. Their day's catch is one large turtle and two Spanish fish, weighing probably 300 pounds. These fish have all been harpooned. No seat or table in the shack. Only one tin mug. They cook over a fire outside using a large turtle back for a dish. I cannot see what they live on. They have three pack mules. All are in poor condition. After the meal one goes for gas for me with a note and an American $10 bill. It is 30 miles to the gas station, which is owned by an Italian.

July 12. They arrive with three tins of gas in an old Ford car. They bring some food, for which I pay 25 pesos. They are well under the influence of alcohol. They carry the gas down to my boat and I get the *Queen Mary* under way. Had it not been for a nor'wester, and had I been able to keep on my course, I would have been 100 miles up the coast.

July 14. I get under way. It is calm all day so I run my engine and make about 35 miles.

Crossing the Gulf of California

July 14. Wind west and a gale. Get in under cape and sleep till about 5 p.m. Togo barks and I look out to find a large fishing boat. They too are seeking shelter from the nor'wester. I go on board and have supper with them and get one dozen fresh eggs. Dark now, so I haul over in a cove and anchor. Wind still west and a gale. Probably made 25 miles. I saved the *Queen Mary* a hard dragging by getting into this harbour, the first since I sailed from Mazatlán.

July 15. Wind high, so I cook a mulligan stew and put in the day repairing sails. At midnight get under way and make a short tack but find too much wind, so make shelter in cove again.

A year gone by

July 16. Wind is more favourable. Start engine and sail up the coast 23 miles. Wind heads me off and I am forced to seek shelter. I am about 40 miles from Cedros Island and 350 miles from San Diego. Wind blowing a gale. I will not get any farther today. I see several fishing boats going east. I am reminded of home. I've been away one year today. What an experience! I reflect on what I have gone through on the Atlantic, the Gulf of Mexico, the Yucatan Channel, the Caribbean Sea, and now the Pacific. No man ever sailed this coast west alone before in a boat as small as this. If I can make it to Vancouver, I will end my voyage. May God grant it so!

My little *Queen Mary* is running along comfortably in a low fog, wind from the south with a fresh breeze, the sun looking through the fog now and then. Togo has the strap on his collar fastened near the companionway. I rely on him being on the look-out. I doze off and let the *Queen Mary* run along with the foresail almost to the knot. Suddenly he awakens me; the hair is standing on his back and his eyes are staring wildly astern. He was in the habit of barking at porpoises, sharks, birds, and dolphins, boat lights, or anything he thought required my attention.

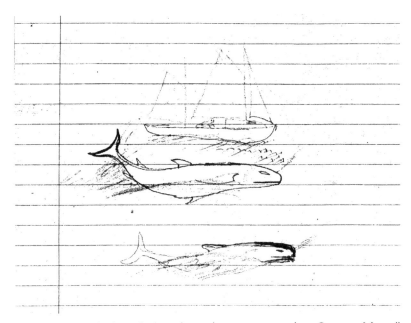

A drawing titled "Whales that almost upset the *Queen Mary*," from Capt. Crowell's logbook.

One look at the surface of the water about 50 yards astern tells me a large whale must have spouted and submerged in short notice. I haul in the foresheet and let down the centreboard at once, preparing to manoeuvre the *Queen Mary*.

A sperm whale or cachalot will usually stay down nine minutes if fishing among a school of herring, but will likely not notice a boat. Before long, far below the surface I see this huge monster gradually come to light. He seems to be out of line off my wake a little to starboard. He comes out of water more than half the length of himself, probably 30 feet from my beam ends—his head and one-third of his body completely clear of the water. His lower jaw is perhaps 15 feet long and leans to the starboard. His underparts are decorated with moss and barnacles, with some sort of suckers or fish clinging to his underside, some dropping off as he rolls toward me. The end of his nose is round and the blow-hole very much in the forward part of his head. A small spout of air going almost directly ahead of his nose shows that this is a sperm whale. It is perhaps 80 feet long, and the largest whale I have ever seen. From the top of his back down over his port side is a scar about 4 feet long. It is in a V-shape and shows white blubber where the black skin has been tom off.

In submerging, this great bulk rolls toward me. The wind and spray from his body offsets the southerly wind in my sail and for a minute I think I am going to have a long stay in Davy Jones's locker. The tail of this monster sways over to port, clearing the heel of the *Queen Mary* by a scant 6 feet. This is not a pleasant situation, and I feel there is more coming.

I am in the act of starting my little Palmer to help me manoeuvre, when Togo jumps or falls in the companionway, hanging himself by the neck during one of the most critical moments of my voyage. My engine requires priming before I could start her, which I have to drop to relieve the dog from his agony.

The whale appears again on the surface, this time on the port side with the end of his crooked jaw almost against the *Queen Mary*. I manoeuvre the boat starboard and windward. The lee of this great body takes the wind from my sails for a minute. I could take an oar and shove the *Queen Mary* from his side, but a second thought and the force of the sea drives me away from a dangerous position. This time he rolls a complete somersault over toward me, but the *Queen Mary* is just a little too fast for him. As he comes back again in position, he shoots ahead and raises his tail out of the water, which sways over the top of my spar, striking the water within a few feet of the *Queen Mary*'s bow, sending tons of water within a few feet and spray over my boat.

What a close call! This last act tells me of his angry condition, for a couple of large sharks pass under the *Queen Mary* and shoot away in his wake. It appears that these sharks are tearing at the blubber from the wound in his side, and he expects to roll against my boat to clean himself of the brutes trying to devour his body.

It looks as though he has turned a complete somersault and

will not be back on such short notice, so I start my engine and throw over gasoline and water from the pump. Whales, particularly sperm whales, will not inhale foul air, the smell of any bilge water or anything else that causes the breath in their air chambers to be foul. They will at once disappear.

I do not have long to wait, for he comes up within a few feet of the stern of my boat and would have lifted me out of the water on the top of his head or taken me sideways in his jaws, but then with the flash of an eye he disappears beneath the surface. I did not see my determined friend again.

Eventually a large fishing boat named *Victoria* comes down the coast. I speak to her and discover she is from San Pedro, bound for the fishing grounds. They heave to and I go alongside for a chat. I see they are eating watermelon. I find out details from the captain about the coastline and they give me all the food I want. They advise me to pull in to Cedros Island as the weather is very bad in the bay. It is now evening and I anchor in shelter of the island and make myself a real beef stew from some fresh beef they gave me. I have tomatoes and fruit.

The whale, the whale, the mighty and free;
But only in size is he the King of the Sea.

Many years ago I was a hand in a large fishing schooner on the Grand Banks, southeast of Newfoundland. In those days a schooner stayed out for perhaps four months, loaded with salt and supplies, 23 men and 20 single dories. They would leave in April and fish on various grounds or banks along the coastline from the Western Banks to the Grand Banks, or even up to Labrador.

On one particular voyage in July, we were anchored in shoal water on Quero Bank. We had a good run of fish; squid bait was plenty with the weather was fine. The whales were fishing the banks in schools, but harmless to the dories. The night was fine and the moon was at its best. The crew had all turned in for the night. I was standing on my one-hour anchor watch, when I heard a whale blow astern, and then a great splash.

I took the night glasses hanging inside the companionway and I put them to my eyes. Less than 100 yards from the schooner, I saw a great battle going on between a whale and a swordfish. I called the captain, and we viewed the battle from the deck.

As the whale has no way of defending himself but to plunge and roll and use his tail, he becomes a sure target if he makes a false move. The swordfish is a little faster than the whale on a straight swim, keeping under the whale's carcass and stabbing him from underneath. The thrasher shark, as many fishermen call them, follows the whale from close range. As the whale comes to the surface, the thrasher jumps in the air and, with the turn of his tail, falls head-down as near to the whale's eyes or blowhole as possible. He keeps the whale under, preventing him from spouting and making the kill easier.

The swordfish is perhaps 300 pounds, with a sword extending about 30 inches out from his nose. It is flat, perhaps 4 inches wide at the base, very sharp at the point, and formed of bone. Swimming with a dash of speed, the swordfish drives his sword in perhaps the whale's oil chamber or as near as possible, rolls around a few times, and prepares for another stab.

The ocean was calm and the light of the moon gave us a clear view of the battle. It only lasted about 30 minutes. During that time, the whale came to the surface four times. During the first three, he had his tail high in the air and with a splash he sent the spray far. The last time he came to the surface, the shark made two more leaps and landed a direct hit, and then it was all over.

The whale groaned. The last time he came slowly to the surface and only showed slight motions of his tail. We knew the battle was over. The whale was dead. Morning broke and we threw our dories out and rowed over to the carcass of this great creature. He was lying underside-up and showing many stabs from the sword of his killer.

July 17. Still lying in the cove at the end of Cedros Island. Gale blowing from the west offshore. I get under way but find the sea terrible. Anchor again in the lee. I am about 100 yards from shore. Herds of seals are around me everywhere. They lie on the beach barking and growling all night. Togo is terribly excited. It is 6:30 p.m. and I am still at anchor. The wind is again northwest and some more boats come to anchor. It looks better for tomorrow. I am terribly lonesome tonight and would like to be home with my family. God bless them and keep them safe.

July 18. Wind moderates, but still from the west. I get under way and this wind seems to draw southwest. I get on my course again for the first time in some two weeks. It is now noon. I make coffee, warm up my beef stew, and have dinner. At about 3, the wind increases fast. I sight land in the north. It's California again. I heave to and let the boat jog, as it is very rough. I stand in the companionway till midnight, and the wind moderates.

July 19. A light breeze comes up from the north and I follow the coast all day. About 4, I sight a small island which I believe to be San Martin, southeast of the cape. I have a nice breeze, close-haul. I make the cape. I make lee again under the island, and anchor. I make fish chowder for supper. I will have to do some repairs on the sails before I leave tomorrow.

July 20. Wind west. I repair my sails. At noon I get under way again. Wind hauls north and comes off a good breeze. The *Queen Mary* skiffs along at her best. Evening, I heave to and let the boat jog to the west. I see many lights off to the west.

July 21. Calm. Get under way. Light wind. Sight a fisherman. He speaks to me. It is the *Victoria*. He gave me a tin of gas, some food, and fresh meat. I sail close-haul. At dark, I heave to. Made about 50 miles.

A lonesome birthday

July 22. My birthday. I am 57 years young. This coast is very rough. In the last 600 miles I have not seen a place to land. No trees or grass. Barren sand hills for miles. Not a road or even a mule's track.

San Diego, California

July 23. I expect to make San Diego today. Breeze north. Use up my tin of gas. Find it very thick on the coast. Pick up the sound of what seems like a large ship blowing for right of way. Find I am with two battleships and submarines. I am now under the west land of San Diego. This is the US Navy base of the Pacific. The fog lifts and I find this ship manoeuvring in the bay. Pilot boat goes by and sings out, "Hello, *Queen Mary*." He directs me in to the yacht club, and there I spend the evening after passing customs.

July 24. I haul over to the Broadway pier. The city's centre has a population of about 180,000. Post office very handy. I write and receive mail. Get myself some clothes. Spend the day talking with people.

July 25. I meet Mrs. Jack Creighton, who once lived in Dartmouth. She has a son and daughter. They drive down and take me to their home. We have dinner and they take me sightseeing. Mrs. Creighton bakes a nice cake for me and then drives me back.

July 26. I move to the San Diego yacht club and meet many new friends. They give me a box of food supplies.

San Pedro, California

July 27. At an early hour I get under way. About 82 miles yet to San Pedro. I pick up a west wind and head tides. Haul in close to the coast. Gasoline tube fills up, so I anchor and do some repairs. Calm, so I start my engine. Finish with 35 miles sailing distance.

July 28. Sail at 6 a.m. Breeze southeast, course northwest. Put over line, lose three salmon and then finally catch one weighing about eight pounds. I lose no time in preparing this fellow for dinner. At 10 a.m., the fog shuts down thick. Find many boats and steamers on the coast. At 1 p.m., I pick up a boat coming out of San Pedro. I see a fairway buoy and go in and anchor at the gas wharf at the foot of Main Street. Go to the post office. Come back, and find a reporter waiting for me. Sell short story to the press. They arrange for me to talk on the radio. Will have boat hauled out here for repairs and new sails made. Meet some people from Nova Scotia. I have dinner with the mayor.

July 29. Haul over to Matt Walsh's shipyard for repairs.

July 30. Fine day. Working on the *Queen Mary*, cleaning and painting. Having a suit of sails made and new garboards put in. Worms had eaten through them. Meet a friend from Nova Scotia and spend a pleasant evening.

July 31. Still working on the *Queen Mary*. Weather fine. Have a cruise around the city. Spend evening at a picture show.

August 1. Spend a quiet day. Do some writing. I must wait several days for my sails.

August 6. Tonight I have an engagement at the American Legion to speak about my voyage. I meet a Mr. Healy, who brings me down supplies. He is a grand old man. At 4 p.m., we launch the *Queen Mary*. Sails come on board and all repairs done. The reporter comes down and takes pictures of the *Queen Mary* as she slides into the water. Matt Walsh does all this work free of charge. I get a wire here from Victoria, British Columbia, saying to come to the Enterprise wharf. Get gas and oil and sail for St. Antonio. Course northwest about 40 miles. Good breeze and, at about 10 p.m., I haul into this summer place. Six reporters are on the dock waiting for me. They want to have my boat taken out of the water for the showground, but I have no time to stop, as the weather will soon be bad.

August 8. I get under way. Thick of fog. Light air north. I run the engine all day. At about 5, I haul in and land. Fog still thick. A lot of kelp on the surface here. I do not do any night sailing. Sailing distance 55 miles.

August 9. Still thick of fog and, at about 10 a.m., I haul in and make Santa Barbara. Large oil field here, so I do not stay. The fog lifts. Large steamer loading oil half a mile from land. Wind west-southwest. At 4 p.m., the wind breezes up, and at dark I anchor again. Sailing distance 55 miles.

August 10. Get under way from a small cove. I had supper with a fisherman named Jack Marrios at his camp. They are fishing for mussels that grow on the rocks. They dive for them and pry them off the rocks with a long knife. The diver throws them in a wire basket, which is hauled to the surface. The mussels weigh from one to two pounds each. Three men work in each boat. They slice the mussels—they look like pieces of salt pork—then ice them and ship them to market. The Japanese also work at this new business; they put the mussels in cans.

There are many new things on this coast. The kelp that grows along here on the shoal rocky bottom is also quite a paying industry. It grows up to the surface in some 10 to 15 fathoms of water, and there are acres of it along the coast. It is almost impossible to shove through it. Many boats take shelter behind these kelp beds from wind and sea. The kelp is cut and put in scows and towed in to factories, where it is made into medicine, food, and other products.

The Japanese seem to have a great hold on this part of the country. They are to be found on farms and operating the vegetable markets in the city. They can also be found working in the fishing industry along the coast, and seem to be successful in their undertakings. For years there has been a lot of salmon fishing in Puget Sound. Ships can be found off Prince Rupert and in Alaskan waters trolling and netting fish all the year around. Some reports here say they are killing the spawning season and should not be allowed in our waters.

I am anchored in a little cove in the lee of some ledges under a lighthouse. It has been thick of fog all day. I have made about 49 miles in the last 12 hours. Togo swims ashore with a card. I get a supper of bacon, eggs, and jam. Fog lifts and I can see the lighthouse. I am about 1 mile from the light. A woman takes the card from Togo. She has been washing her children on the sand beach. She takes a child under each arm and runs across the beach. I see her no more.

August 12. There seems to be duck about these ledges. I drop what looks like a good fat one, and Togo brings him aboard. I start my engine. It is thick of fog. I pick up the sound of machinery close on starboard. I haul in and make the end of the Standard Oil wharf. Here a large Norwegian steamer is loading oil. I go aboard and they give me bread, potatoes, and corned beef. I fill my water tanks and get five gallons of gas. I get under way and start my engine. It is calm. Anchor in 6 fathoms of water. Distance of 40 miles. My duck from early morning is put in a pot. Togo watches my every move, as he is interested in eating.

August 13. Good breeze south. Sail all day. At about 5, the wind dies out. Start engine and go in under land. I cannot run as floating weeds are too bad.

San Francisco, California

August 14. Get under way early. Light breeze from the south. Probably 70 miles from San Francisco. I make a good day's run, and go under the Golden Gate Bridge. Tie up at the yacht club. I am flooded with memories of bygone days. I thank God, who has so safely piloted me over this long and dangerous voyage. As I look over the remainder of my voyage to Vancouver, I feel that the same pilot will carry me on to the end. I meet many friends at this yacht club. They invite me to stay at the club, but I remain on the *Queen Mary.*

August 15. I receive a royal welcome here. They feel this is the longest voyage ever made by one lone navigator, in the smallest foreign craft ever to enter San Francisco's harbour.

August 16. Very busy day at the mayor's office.

August 18. Go to Madden shipyard and have boat repaired. Find that the owner is the mayor of the city.

August 19. Return to yacht basin. Receive a box of supplies from the captain and then go to the Chamber of Commerce and meet Mr. William Mauer, a shipowner from San Francisco. He takes me sightseeing. We visit many historical places around the bay and go over the Golden Gate Bridge, which opened in 1937.

August 20. Mr. Mauer has my eyes tested and gives me glasses as a present.

August 21. Go down to the pier and meet a lot of the boys fishing along the coast.

August 22. Busy day at yacht basin.

August 23. Take in supplies and gas.

Eureka, California

August 24. Sail at 10:30 a.m. for Eureka. Fresh breeze all day. I heave to at about 8 p.m. Sailing distance 45 miles.

August 25. Wind fair. Course northwest by west. Sail till 8:30. Heave to.

August 26. Wind south. Fog. Stiff breeze all day. Put over line and catch small salmon. Salmon for supper. At about 6, wind moderates and fog thick. Heave to and cook potatoes.

August 27. Speak to some fishing boats. They are salmon fishing and report a small season.

August 28. Wind northwest and heavy. Get in under land and anchor.

August 29. Get an early start. Close-haul up the coast, and very rough. Probably 30 miles from Eureka. My foresail is carried away. A fishing boat comes up alongside and throws me a line and tows me in under land. I anchor and repair my rigging. Get under way and go into Eureka. Make a fire and dry the cabin. Salmon for supper.

August 30. I am lying at Young's slip. I take in supplies. The sun is shining. I dry my clothes and get ready for the sea again.

Reach Coos Bay

August 31. Sail at 10:30. Thick of fog and very rough. I get out over the bar and sail up the coast northwest by north. By evening I have sailed about 30 miles. Heave to. A bad night.

September 1. Wind is southeast. Breeze is good. Course still northwest by north. Get under way at 5 a.m. I must be near

Cape Blanco. Haul in and sail two hours. Heave to and listen for fog alarm. Have 8 fathoms of water. Pick up sound of alarm and judge I am 4 miles east of the cape. Sea very rough and uneven, so I keep off again. The fog lifts a little and I see some buildings. I tack, stand off, and start my engine. Will make shelter in the lee of some large ledges. The lifeguard sees me and sends out a search boat just as I am comfortably anchored. They tell me I am not in a safe anchorage. The wind is fair, and I have anchored here to make a cup of coffee and sleep for a few hours. At 5:30 p.m., they tow me to the Coos Bay station. I anchor for the night.

September 2. I rest all day and have dinner at the home of Officer Wilson and his family. A good night's sleep.

September 3. I am given gas and supplies. At about 3 p.m., I put to sea again. A light air north. I sail down the coast and anchor about 275 miles east of Cape Flattery. The night is fine.

September 4. Thick of fog. I catch another fine salmon. Wind light south. On course. At 4, I am in sight of a small boat harbour. I plan on going in for the night. Start engine; connecting rod breaks. I go in and find this place to be Depoe Bay, Oregon.

September 5. Have engine repaired. There are perhaps 30 salmon boats fishing out of this bay. The entrance is only 40 feet wide.

September 6. Wind is light but the tide is in my favour. Looks like a nor'wester, so at about 5 I haul in under land and anchor in the shelter of a cliff. Fishermen dread northwest wind on this coast. There are no harbours for many miles. Have sailed about 30 miles today. Boil corned salmon and potatoes and eat with pickles. Togo and I have a good supper and sleep.

September 7. Wind ahead and going bad. I make some 20 miles when I have to go under land again. Wind is northwest by north but I am in a sheltered spot along with some other fishing boats. At noon I take out the last corned beef and make stew. Many salmon fishermen along this coast but harbours are poor, mostly bar harbours. The coastline is very rough. It more like Nova Scotia's coast.

September 8. Get under way at 3 a.m. Wind is light from the north. I am on course. Toward evening the wind moderates, so I start my engine and go into a small harbour.

September 9. Take in supplies and then head out again in company with boats all day. It is smooth. I let the *Queen Mary* jog; I have bacon, plenty of fish heads, and coffee. Sail till midnight.

The home stretch

September 10. Get under way at about 9 and sight the Cape Flattery lighthouse in Washington. I start my engine and get in at about 5:30 p.m. I thank God. I am tired of this voyage.

September 11. I clean up the *Queen Mary* and sail for Victoria, which is about 25 miles. I reach Victoria at about 5:30 p.m. I receive a great reception. They have arranged for the *Queen Mary* to be put on display at the provincial exhibition.

September 11–18. The *Queen Mary* is on display at the fairgrounds. I speak at the yacht club to about 130 members. Have a cruise on Harry Barnes's yacht.

Reaching my goal

September 22. I sail for Vancouver·

September 24. I arrive at noon in Vancouver. I tie up at the Royal

Royal Vancouver Yacht Club

3811 POINT GREY ROAD
VANCOUVER, B. C.

407 West Cordova St.,

November 12, 1937.

Captain William A. Crowell,
570 Hornby St.,
Vancouver, B. C.

Dear Captain Crowell:

On behalf of the Commodore and sailing members of the Royal Vancouver Yacht Club, we wish to tender you herewith our cheque in the sum of $45.00, as a slight token of our appreciation for the wonderful sailing fete which you so recently accomplished and about which we had the pleasure of hearing from you at our recent dinner.

The boys in the Club are still talking about this demonstration of what can be done by a man who is fortified with courage and desire to attain the goal to which he set out.

I attach hereto a list of those who appreciated your accomplishment sufficiently to volunteer adding their name to the list which made up the enclosed cheque.

We all wish you the most pleasant of trips home, and will be very glad indeed to hear from you as to how you progress upon your arrival in Halifax. If and when you do finish your book on this trip, please advise this Club, as I know a great number of us would want to purchase a copy.

Yours very sincerely,

Harold A. Jones,
Fleet Captain, R.V.Y.C.

A thank-you letter from the Royal Vancouver Yacht Club.

Vancouver Yacht Club. My voyage on the *Queen Mary* that started in Halifax on July 16, 1936, comes to an end. I reflect on the determination that was required in sailing such a long voyage. It was daunting, and many times I was discouraged.

All seamen understand the many things that can happen on short notice when on the seas. We are well trained in handling sheet and sail, but we also know we are largely at the mercy of the hand of fate.

REMAINING DAYS
ON LAND AND AT SEA

After returning home from my long voyage to Vancouver, I cleaned the *Queen Mary* and sailed around the coast of Nova Scotia, fished, and then got her ready for the Canadian National Exhibition in Toronto in September of 1938.

It is a long sail from Nova Scotia to Ontario, but with my 3-horsepower Palmer engine I felt I could get through the narrow waters and tides of the St. Lawrence Seaway. I sailed on the first of August. The fair is held early in September and I knew I would have many stops. I needed plenty of time to go down the Nova Scotia coast and through the Strait of Canso to Charlottetown, Prince Edward Island. I sailed at noon and made a few miles west under power. Late in the afternoon, the gas tank sprang a leak. I stopped the engine, hoisted my sails, and went into Summerside, PEI. I met the mayor and council and they made arrangements for me to speak at Holman's Department Store.

From there I sailed to the fair in Pictou, Nova Scotia, to mark the end of the lobster season. They made arrangements to have my boat in the parade. I met the High Line Fishermen of the Season and also the Honourable Angus Macdonald, premier of Nova Scotia.

Sailing away from Pictou, I headed up the coast and across to Cape Perce. There was no harbour for anchorage, so I made fast to the side of a wharf late in the afternoon with a light southwest wind. I wrote and met friends. I had been there many years ago as a boy. At 3 a.m., I found my *Queen Mary* trying to jump up on the wharf. The wind had moved quickly to the southeast. It was dark and raining, but I had to get away from there and look for shelter.

As the wind was giving me a fair run, I decided to sail as far as Goose Bay. I hoisted the foresail and was soon on my way. As daylight broke, I found myself at the entrance of Goose Bay. It was thick of fog and raining and as nice a sou'easter coming on as you would want. With the tide running out the bay and the gale from the southeast, the going looked bad.

I sighted a small fishing boat getting her anchor. I decided to tack and speak to him. Togo came on deck to look at the fishing boat, and the next sea swept him overboard. I tried to pick him up in all that sea. I carried a dip net with me, which I used for many purposes, and this time it helped me to land him. By this time I was out of sight of the other boat. Just as I got on my course again, a large white freighter appeared, coming out of Goose Bay and loaded with pulpwood piled 10 feet high. It was in the act of swinging on her course. By the time I came head to the wind by tacking, he was dangerously close to me. To make matters worse, she rolled toward me and let go of a bunch of pulpwood, perhaps a thousand pieces. Any of those pieces could have gone right through the *Queen Mary*. The close call left me in a raft of pulpwood. Before and after that I had many close calls, by Davy, but, by faith and good judgment, I survived. After 35 days of headwinds and tide I arrived in Toronto. I went to the Royal Canadian Yacht Club, but was disappointed by the hospitality they showed me.

I was met by one of their boats under sail out in the lake and received a card of welcome to their club, but still I found that they were not the same boat-minded seagoing yachtsmen we have on the east coast. Over half the members had never been in anything other than a rowboat or a canoe. I never stepped inside of any of their boat clubs, nor had an invitation to take part in a weekend social event. I remained a few days tied up at their little dock. I did receive a visit from the commodore and some of the club officials.

At last came the opening of the exhibition on September 8.

I had called the exhibition committee. They had a place for my boat and also wanted to see Togo. I received a glad hand, but since they wanted 45 per cent of my earnings, I did not place the *Queen Mary* on the exhibition grounds. Instead, I got a permit from the Harbour Board to lie at the seawall going into the exhibition grounds. This, of course, was much better for me, as my boat remained in the water. I tied up at the seawall and opened for business. My little *Queen Mary* and my dog were part of the water attractions, but the police came down with orders for me to leave, as they were not getting any revenue from my work.

I moved to the Toronto dock, or the city dock. One day after a big crowd had gathered around, including many children, Togo performed on a little stand on the bow of the *Queen Mary*. While he was entertaining the children, the crowd kept shoving forward and, in the process, pushed a small boy of perhaps seven off the wharf. He struck his head, and sank. I did not see him fall, but the screams from the crowd attracted my attention. Someone on the wharf called out, "A boy fell overboard!" I jumped to the scow and then, feet-first, jumped over as close to where he sank as I could.

It was fresh water and very dark. I could not see my hand before my eyes. I only descended a few feet, as there was 16 feet of water, but I did not reach the bottom. As I made a stroke to get back to the surface, my hand touched the boy's leg. I picked him up and brought him to the surface. Within a few minutes I had him on the scow, where he received good care. After about 20 minutes, I called out for his mother. Some of the people cried out, "You distinguished yourself, Captain. With your quick action you saved this boy's life." News travels fast and within a few minutes I had many from the press asking for a story. But as I never cared much for that kind of publicity, I told them that I would take my glory with me. Time marches on.

Another day, I was lying at the city dock one afternoon when a squall of wind came in without much notice. Probably 1,000 people were standing waiting nearby for a passenger ship to come in. The squall blew many of the hats off the heads in the crowd, and they landed in the water a few feet from the dock. Togo had been working with me on the *Queen Mary*'s deck, so I showed him the hats by throwing little rocks at them. He dove off the dock, from a height of perhaps 10 feet, picked up the hats, and swam them to where I could reach them and pass them back to their owners. He swam in with seven hats. For his work, the owners left him perhaps $2. Just before dark, a man came along and said, "Captain, there is a lady's large hat floating off the dock. I can see the rim." I called Togo. He jumped in and brought the beautiful hat to the dock to dry. Not long after a car drove down and a beautiful woman got out and said, "Captain, did your dog pick up a hat late this afternoon?" I gave the woman her hat and she didn't even thank me or Togo. She just drove off, without even giving a nickel for an ice cream treat for Togo.

While we were at the Toronto exhibition, Togo entertained thousands of children. He loved to play for them. During our voyage, he entertained children many countries for free. I never charged hospitals or schools for his performances.

After cruising with me for six years, Togo developed head trouble and started to shake his head. Then he started to have fits or weak spells. I had him examined in Vancouver and in Boston. He gradually became worse. The doctors decided he had broken his eardrums. I had him operated on, but he did not get better. He gradually went blind and seemed to be in great pain. The hour eventually came when I had to part with man's best friend. In my writing I cannot do him justice, as he could do the most surprising things. People who saw him called him the most intelligent dog in Canada.

After leaving the Toronto fair, I sailed home through the lakes and through the Welland Canal, connecting Lake Ontario and Lake Erie. From there, I visited Buffalo, went down through the canals, and made many stops along the Hudson River. I went to the White Star Docks at the West, where I had the chance to board the great *Queen Mary* again. I spent a pleasant time on that ship and was given a royal time by the ship's officers, but the ship's former captain, Sir Edgar T. Britten, had since died.

The Gloucester races

I sailed for Gloucester in October 1938 to take part in the races between the *Bluenose*, the world's greatest Grand Banks fishing schooner, and the American fishing schooner, *Gertrude L. Thibault*. Nobody expected me to be at the course in my little sailboat. I had sailed around by way of the St. Lawrence and down through the Hudson River. I was there for the finish of the races and had the honour of speaking on the radio from the deck of both schooners. My boat was the smallest to have ever attended the fishermen's races from any part of the world. I was given a great reception at the races and also as guest at the farewell party for the *Bluenose* and her worthy crew.

I sailed across the Bay of Fundy on the *Bluenose* as one of the crew. My *Queen Mary* sat on her deck. As a member of the crew I took my trick at the wheel and enjoyed steering this schooner very much. It was the fastest and easiest under sail I had ever steered.

When I left the *Bluenose* and stepped down into the *Queen Mary*, I gazed back at her beautiful, graceful lines and her tall spars and thought of the shipbuilders in Lunenburg who had created this perfect ship—the undefeated Grand Banks fishing vessel—never again to be challenged.

Abandoned trip to Sable Island

In the summer of 1939, I fitted out for a cruise to Sable Island, the place known as the graveyard of the Atlantic for the great number of shipwrecks that occurred nearby. Early in September, with a fine morning wind, I set out. At 9 p.m., I had made some 40 miles, when thick fog shut in, leaving me drifting all night.

The next morning the fog was still thick. At 10 a.m., I heard motors running. The noise came from the northwest. Thirty minutes later, the fog lifted just a strip and, some 2 miles from me on the surface, lay a German submarine with its crew on deck. Apparently I had seen them first, as I had a bearing from the sound of their motors, but in a few minutes they spied me and turned their glasses on me. Some 12 crew came up and passed the glasses from one to the other. As the fog lifted farther to the northwest, they sighted another ship, perhaps 5 miles away. I could not see what it was at the time, but within a few minutes all went below, and that was the last I saw of them.

At noon the wind came in from the southeast and I stood in on the land. I arrived in Ship Harbour late that night, and abandoned my cruise to Sable Island. I sailed back to Halifax and finished the season sailing the coast and inland waters. In the fall I hauled the *Queen Mary* out and quietly remained on shore for the next three years.

Remodelling the *Queen Mary*

In 1943, I felt the roar of the sea again. I looked over my little *Queen* to see what changes I could make to her accommodations for a long voyage to the Pacific and Pearl Harbor, Hawaii. For this voyage I remodelled her by putting in new timbers and making her 5 inches deeper. I also put on a little cabin in which I had enough headroom to sit on a stool 10 inches high. As I remodelled her during the winter of 1944, many people came to talk and see my work. "Where are you going this time?" they asked. News got out that this voyage would close the pages of my story.

I decided to take out my steel centreboard and box, put in a new engine, and cut down her spar and sail plan. Engine troubles prevented me from sailing till 1947. When I finally sailed my little *Queen Mary* out of Halifax, it was for the last time. I would never sail her back home. On my departure, about 1,000 people waved and wished me bon voyage. They also advised me not to go. I later discovered they were right. I made a rough crossing of the Bay of

Fundy. There was a fresh southerly and a bad sea. By removing the *Queen Mary*'s steel centreboard I had changed my trusty sailboat into a helpless sea boat. She would not lie to, nor head reach. At daylight, the night wind was over and I was 6 miles south of Bar Harbor, Maine.

At 9 a.m., a plane flew over me and dropped a message: "If you want assistance, haul down your front sail." The message is now among my treasures. The sea had broken over my engine room during the night and my little *Queen* was almost unmanageable. The Coast Guard had come out from the southwest harbour, wanting to tow me in to spend the weekend with them. After telling them I was not in distress, I accepted their offer and spent the next three days with them. I admire that they are always ready to give assistance, are well trained, and have good boats and equipment. They deserve and are worthy of all the trust that Uncle Sam places in them.

While sailing along the east coast of the United States for the next three months, I made up my mind that my boat was no longer a trusty craft and that she could not again sail me to the Pacific. On my arrival at Miami, Florida, I met my wife, and we spent the next month together. On her advice and the advice of port officials, I changed my course to the Bahamas. Early in February 1948, I sailed to the Bahamas.

Sailing from the coast of Florida, the wind was light from the west. But within a few miles of Bimini, the westernmost part of the Bahamas, the wind jumped northeast and brought a thunderstorm. Next a gale blew from the northeast, and gave me another frightful night, probably worse than the night in the Bay of Fundy. The only thing that saved me from being lost that night, along with a couple of fishing boats, was the strong tide running northeast against the wind.

Being close to some of the low reefs in shoal water, I had a bad night. I was glad to see the cold grey morning. I am sure my boat jumped 12 feet from the breaking crest of one sea to the other.

She landed on her bottom again and moved every board, except the engine head. When I finally got my bearings, it was a Sunday morning. I was within 3 miles of Bimini and to windward. I lowered my small reef foresail that I had been trying to lie to under and hoisted my jib and ran down to the entrance of Bimini harbour. I anchored, warmed up my engine, and entered. I spent the next week with people from the area and the island's commissioner. They could not believe that I had crossed the Gulf Stream that night. Many people did not believe the long sailing and the many gales that I rode out in my little *Queen Mary*.

The end of my sailing days

After a week's rest in Bimini, I cleared for Nassau. On this last passage I visited Bird Key Island, where I spent three days waiting for a sou'easter to blow out. I was not feeling well. I still hadn't gotten over the bad storm in the Gulf and the way my little *Queen Mary* had tossed me around during that gale.

Sailing from Bird Key to Nassau I lost one of my motor blades and could not use power. This gave me an extra night out. During the last eight hours of this voyage, with a strong headwind, I passed out. For hours the little *Queen* sailed on. Just before dark I came to again and found that I was in 5 fathoms of water and within 1 mile of the breakers west of the western entrance to Nassau harbour. I anchored for the night.

I was very dizzy and had to keep hold of something to get around. I fell partway over the side of the boat with one arm dangling in the water, but got myself back in and rode out the night in my little bunk. The *Queen* rode on with no light, no watch. At least two fishermen were close by me and reported my position. In the morning I was able to get under way and made it to the customs office. My sailing days were over.

I spent some five weeks on the island. I knew that I was unable to sail my boat home. I dismantled her and shipped her back home on a large ship; I had to pay $680. During my long stay in

Capt. Crowell and his daughter, Helen (Frank Crowell Leaman's mother).

what felt like no man's land, I spent a lot of time at the hospital.

I expect to see my little *Queen Mary* in sailing trim again. I believe she is the greatest little sea boat that ever travelled by the hand of a fisherman. I live in hope that I will have her rigged again in all her glory.

On a fine morning in Nassau, I said goodbye to the little craft that had carried me so many miles, climbed on board a Pan-American clipper, and flew home.

Now as I sail my memory only
As the seas break on the shore
And the many ships that passed by night
Will not pass me anymore.
Long nights passed by with seas and gales
While God protected me.

Last port

The old saying "You can't keep a good man down" also refers to wooden ships. However, it is also true that time marches on and finds our ship's timbers weak. In humans these weak timbers, unfortunately, cannot be replaced. But in a ship they can be fixed. In my boat shop, where once I had carefully fitted every plank and every timber with my own hands, I hope to make the *Queen Mary* new again.

In closing my book, I take time to remember all those along my sea voyages who not only threw me a towline but reached down and gave me money that helped me buy supplies and helped build up my courage to sail on. May they all, with their snow-white sails, find a place of rest and happiness where the calm waters and gentle trade winds blow. I pray that their anchors hold them in peace and happiness for the rest of their days.

I have asked my grandson, Frank, if he desires a life at sea. "Pa," he said to me, "if in later years I am called to defend our nation's flag, it will be in the Navy."

Just as my grandfather left me his sea chest, I will leave one to my grandson. It will be more streamlined, and I hope he never has to use it out at sea—instead, it will be a memory of me and my seafaring days.

We courageous seamen of days gone by had no fear of sea or gales or diseases. We never failed to carry on. We had to. We had no choice.

A GRANDSON REMEMBERS

In the late 1950s, I loved spending time at my grandparents' big wooden house on Erskine Street in downtown Dartmouth. After the school bell rang at the end of the day, I'd walk from Bicentennial Junior High School to my grandparents' house. My grandfather was usually out in the small shipyard he had built behind the house and inside one of his boats-in-progress. The smell of tarred rope, creosote, and wood chips greeted my arrival. He would be waiting for me, eager to have help with the clinching on one of the beautiful lapstreak boats he was making. Lapstreak, I learned, is a method of boat building in which the edges of hull planks overlap. The planks are joined, end to end, into a strake. Developed in northern Europe, the lapstreak technique was used by the Vikings.

As my grandfather got older and his sore leg and arm bothered him too much to get under the boat himself, he would send me there. Crawling under the boat, I would hold up the planks while he clinched the nail. He would pay me 25 cents for my work. After we were done for the day, I'd head to the corner store to buy a Big 8 cola, a chocolate bar, and bag of chips with my earnings.

My grandfather's small shipyard had everything we needed to build a boat: ribs and stem posts, stern transoms and rudders, bits for drilling holes, planes, chisels, clamps, glue pots, paint, varnish, and plenty of turpentine—he was crazy for turpentine. He was like a magician: building boats, houses, and furniture without blueprints, making me believe that a man could do anything he set his mind to.

My grandfather seemed to be capable of making anything

with his hands. He made building a boat exciting. We used primitive methods, shaping wood by first steaming it in an old drainpipe: the wood was placed in the pipe, a fire was lit below, and water was poured into the pipe to create steam. The wood stayed in the pipe with the steam till it warped, then it was taken out and shaped.

When I wasn't helping my grandfather in his shipyard, I'd be inside his house. My favourite place was his den, a private room on the main floor. My grandmother didn't dare go in there, and I felt privileged that he opened the door to me. To an 11-year-old boy, that den was like Aladdin's cave. Whalebones hung on the wall, along with curiosities from around the world. I sometimes sat on a chair made from a whale's vertebrae. I was in awe of the seahorses he had set on a shelf in an old net. Even though I could touch them, I didn't really believe they existed in the ocean. Small model ships that my grandfather had built filled every spare space. He flipped through mail-order catalogues to find the ships—kits complete with figurines and equipment—ordered them, and waited patiently until they arrived by mail. I sat for hours and watched him build model ships. My job was to pass him the intricate pieces of his puzzle.

On one wall of the den hung a 3-foot-high map showing the locations of the hundreds of shipwrecks near Sable Island, a small stretch of land located in the ocean southeast of Halifax. As many as 350 vessels are thought to have been wrecked by the island's sandbars. Frequent thick fog, treacherous currents, and the island's location in the middle of rich fishing grounds and a major transatlantic shipping route made it a dangerous spot. Looking at the map, I dreamed of going to the island one day to witness where so many ships had been lost.

Exciting adventure books lined the shelves, along with duck decoys, fishing rods, and trout and salmon flies. My grandfather loved to fish and hunt and also to collect firearms. My favourite was his old Brown Bess, a type of gun used in the American Rev-

Capt. Crowell after a successful hunting trip.

olution, which hung on the wall. I never found out where it came from. All he said was that some of his relatives on the Eastern Shore had given it to him.

The Dartmouth Fish and Game Protective Association, which promoted conservation and responsible hunting, was my grandfather's favourite charity. I had no idea that my grandfather was an early environmentalist like Farley Mowat and David Suzuki. A priority for the association was educating people about the dangers of forest fires. I remember going to what seemed like every school and community hall in the area and putting up Smokey Bear posters with slogans like "Remember: Only You Can Prevent Forest Fires." My grandfather built boats for the association to raffle off and produced its float for Dartmouth's Natal Day parade every August. In most parades, I had to stand on the float he'd built. Sometimes I'd hold a gun with a sign behind me that read: "Carry out your dead deer and not your dear friend."

I inherited my grandfather's love of fishing but not his love of hunting. After shooting a deer once, I felt sick, and never tried it again. But I did learn to snare rabbits and skin them. If I objected to skinning rabbits—or any other task—my grandfather would respond with his oft-repeated saying: "Grandson, the sooner you do what I tell you, the sooner you'll be a man." As my grandparents ate a lot of rabbit stew, it wasn't uncommon to find rabbits hanging behind their house on a clothesline or deer hanging from the garage rafters.

My grandfather hated idleness. We were expected to be doing something to help our community at all times. At Christmas, we decorated the Grace United Baptist Church, where he was a faithful parishioner, with evergreen boughs and old-fashioned decorations like ribbons and crepe paper. I didn't dare tell him I thought the more modern decorations from the department store looked better. I never wanted to get on his bad side. One time, when he was raising money for a camp for underprivileged kids at Rainbow Haven Beach Provincial Park, not far from Dartmouth, he gave me $5 to give to the camp. Instead, I took the money and went to the movies. When he found out, I got such an earful I never did anything like that again.

My grandfather often gave talks about his trips through Central and South America at the Somme Branch Legion in Dartmouth. He also spoke to students at local schools and was interviewed on television. He even appeared on Max Ferguson's nightly CBC Halifax program *Gazette*.

On special occasions, my grandfather took me to an evening wrestling match at the Dartmouth Arena to watch wrestlers like the Cuban Assassin, Gorgeous George, and Sweet Daddy Siki. I remember the horribly uncomfortable wooden chairs we'd sit in and how they splintered and broke when a wrestler was thrown from the ring.

The Masked Marvel was one of the more entertaining wrestlers. One time he pulled a bottle cap from his trunks to cut the good guy, and the crowd went wild. Everyone, including my grandfather, thought he was really going to do it. On that particular night, my grandfather had paid 50 cents extra for us to sit ringside, and he decided to take matters into his own hands.

When the Masked Marvel flew out of the ring, my grandfather jumped from his seat and berated the wrestler. Another time, he was so angry about the match that he kicked one of the wrestlers in the rear end. The cops had to come and calm him down. When I was older, his behaviour embarrassed me, so I stopped going to wrestling matches with him. But if he were alive today and asked me to go, I wouldn't hesitate. I'd let him have his fun.

My grandfather was often the life of a party. Whether he was quoting the poetry of Lord Alfred Tennyson or Bliss Carman, dancing, or playing the tambourine, he drew people to him. "The sea never changes and its works, for all the talk of men, are wrapped in mystery," I can still hear him quoting Joseph Conrad. He also loved to sing folk songs. When Nova Scotian folklorist Helen Creighton was gathering songs for a collection, he recited "She sailed in the low lands low" to her. Over several decades, Creighton collected over 4,000 traditional songs, stories, and myths. My grandfather was proud to have helped her.

The *Queen Mary*'s Viking funeral

When my grandfather died in 1959, I felt a sense of duty to protect and honour his *Queen Mary*. My grandfather had lovingly built her with his hands and she, in return, had provided him with a vehicle to reach distant lands and the means to chase an elusive freedom. She had protected him during his long voyages and brought him safely back. By preserving her, I would be saving an integral part of my grandfather's life and my family's history.

We took the *Queen Mary* from his backyard boatyard and hauled her along the coast to Buccaneer's Lodge, Motel, and Cottages in East Chester. My family had owned and operated Buccaneer's for close to 40 years, until we sold it in the 1980s. Avid anglers and hunters from New England and the northeastern United States flocked to Nova Scotia's South Shore area, where our rustic lodge was located, drawn by stories of an ocean filled with bluefin tuna and salmon, and pristine woods populated with

A fishing trip at Buccaneers Lodge. Capt. Crowell is in the foreground (wearing a hat); his son-in-law, Frank M. Leaman, and grandson, Frank Crowell Leaman, are at his right.

moose and game birds. Many families returned annually, staying in the same cabin and eating at their regular table in the dining room overlooking Mahone Bay. During the summer months, vacationers came to stay at our popular, rustic lodge, initially called the Owls Head Tuna Camp. Designed by Philip Hooper Moore, an American who established White Point Beach Resort in 1928, Buccaneer's was a horizontal log construction built from locally cut, spruce logs. While our lodge is no longer, White Point remains one of the province's most popular resorts today.

I couldn't think of a better place than Buccaneer's Lodge for the final resting place of the *Queen Mary*. Placed outside the lodge, she could be admired instead of being hidden away in a shed, and forgotten. She would also be close to my family. I envisioned placing my grandfather's model ships and other seafaring artifacts inside the lodge's living room on the central stone fireplace's mantle and framed by two giant tuna tails.

My plans were never realized. One spring morning in the late 1960s my father got a call from the local fire department. He was at home in Dartmouth; the lodge hadn't yet opened for the season and the *Queen Mary* was resting on the lodge's property, surrounded by tall, dry grass. Someone set the grass around her on fire and it didn't take long before her tindery boards were consumed. I didn't see her burn, but I imagined a funeral pyre as if part of an ancient funeral rite, maybe a Viking funeral—I once read that Viking funerals often included cremating the deceased on a pyre in a ship. Fitting, I thought, that this brave craft, which had navigated her way through thousands of miles of reefs, storms, and mishaps, would succumb to a Viking-type funeral in her native land. How would my grandfather have reacted to her death? Knowing that his unwavering philosophy was to carry on no matter what, I concluded that he might have remained silent about her end.

Preserving Nova Scotia's history

I have been on and around the Atlantic Ocean all my life. For decades, my father and I ran fishing and boat tours on a 45-foot cruiser out of the Buccaneer's Lodge, Motel, and Cottages in East Chester. Unlike my grandfather, though, I have always relied on the sounds of bell buoys in the fog or a compass in my hand to return me safely home. I was never brave enough to try something like his great adventure. Surrounded by sailors, ship owners, and fishermen, and listening to gripping tales of storms at sea, treasure islands, and abundant fishing grounds, however, I became a crusader for preserving Nova Scotia's history—a history entwined with the sea.

My interest led me to the *Titanic*. For some who were aboard the ill-fated ship, their tragic stories end in Halifax; many are buried in the city's cemeteries. Five days after the RMS *Titanic* struck a giant iceberg and sank on her maiden voyage, the first of four Canadian vessels went to look for bodies. The Halifax-based cable steamer *Mackay-Bennett* arrived at the site on April 20, 1912, and spent five days recovering 306 bodies, 116 of which were buried at sea. She was relieved by the *Minia*, a Halifax-based cable ship. After eight days of searching, the *Minia* found 17 bodies, two of which were buried at sea.

On May 6, the CGS *Montmagny* left Halifax; it recovered four bodies, one of which was buried at sea. The fourth and final ship in the recovery effort was the SS *Algerine*, which sailed from St. John's, Newfoundland and Labrador, on May 16. It found one body, and took it to Halifax. Only 59 of the recovered bodies were shipped by train to their families. According to the Maritime Museum of the Atlantic, the others bodies were buried in three Halifax cemeteries.

Most of the gravestones, erected in the fall of 1912, are plain granite blocks. In some cases, however, families, friends, or other groups commissioned a larger and more elaborate gravestone. The more personalized graves, including a monument to the "unknown child," are located at Fairview Lawn Cemetery, Halifax.

I have gathered a small collection of *Titanic* memorabilia, including a piece of coal believed to be from the ship. My collection caught the interest of some local businessmen, who asked me to become curator of a *Titanic* society they had formed. The timing coincided with the release of *Titanic*, the 1997 American romantic disaster film. With the society's encouragement, I opened a *Titanic* exhibit at MacDonald House, which sits atop a hill overlooking Lawrencetown Beach. The museum was open for one summer, but it closed due to a lack of funds. Visitors to Halifax can now visit an impressive *Titanic* exhibit at the Maritime Museum of the Atlantic, which includes the shoes of a young male passenger dubbed the "unknown child."

My small *Titanic* exhibit may have closed, but my interest in preserving Nova Scotia's history remained strong. I was also motivated to find a home for my grandfather's nautical belongings, including his model *Queen Mary*. With the encouragement of family and friends, I approached the Maritime Museum of the Atlantic with my grandfather's story, the model *Queen Mary*, and his nautical history collection. I had long admired the museum's devotion to educating the public and presenting priceless historical artifacts, and I felt that my grandfather would have approved. Unknown to me, the museum was planning a "Days of Sail" exhibit, about Nova Scotia's golden age, when shipbuilding and the salt cod trade had brought power and prestige to the province. The museum would feature the story of the *Bluenose*, Canada's legendary Grand Banks schooner, and four epic tales of solo sailing. Valerie Lenethen, the museum's registrar from 1985 to 2000, felt that my grandfather's solo sailing adventures illustrated that important period in Nova Scotia's history.

Each time I met with Valerie, she'd ask, "What else do you have?" She wanted as much information and documentation about my grandfather's life as I could find. I kept digging and bringing more photographs and written material for the exhibit. She also asked if I could bring a photograph of my grandmother and mother. I asked why, since they weren't on my grandfather's solo voyage. "Oh yes," she responded, "but they had the important job of looking after the homefront while he was gone." Their photograph is part of the exhibit; I thank Valerie for reminding me of their valuable role.

I have always been a superstitious person and, throughout this research, I felt my grandfather's presence in the museum. I knew in my heart that I was doing what my grandfather wanted me to do. Valerie understood this too.

My Loyalist family history

In researching my grandfather's life, I went back until I reached the Loyalists. In the Provincial Archives of New Brunswick, I found an important piece of the Crowell family's story. In 1887, William Stryker, Adjutant-General of New Jersey, compiled

Certification that Frank Crowell Leaman is a descendant of Capt. Joseph Crowell.

a history of the New Jersey Volunteers, men he called Loyalists in the American Revolutionary War. As I scanned through this historical document, I found mention of a Captain Joseph Crowell. Putting the pieces together of my family's lineage, I discovered he was my great-great-great-great-grandfather.

According to Stryker, Joseph Crowell was a captain in the Fifth Battalion in 1776. Three years later, he became a captain in the First Battalion. At the time of the Revolutionary War, Captain Crowell ran a farm in Middletown, Monmouth County, New Jersey. Because he was a captain of a local militia, American rebels came calling and asked him to swear allegiance to them. He refused. On March 22, 1779, his property was confiscated, and sold. On one occasion, he was ordered to execute an officer who had never been tried. But, according to Stryker's history, the order was countermanded in the wake of significant protest.

Loyal to the British, Captain Crowell had to get his family out of the United States to safety shortly before what became known as Evacuation Day. On November 25, 1783, the last vestige of British authority in the United States departed New York. It was after this evacuation that General George Washington led the Continental Army triumphantly through town. The last shot of the war was reported to have been fired on this day. A British gunner fired a cannon at crowds gathered on the shore of Staten Island as his ship passed through the mouth of New York harbour.

A few months earlier, late in the summer of 1783, Captain Crowell and his family boarded the *Duke of Richmond* and set sail for British North America, now called Canada. They were among the 669 passengers on board who arrived in Saint John, New Brunswick, on September 27 of that year. Their arrival was a less than a month after the Treaty of Paris was signed on September 3, ending the war.

Little else is known about Captain Joseph Crowell's life, except that he died in New Brunswick. Members of the Crowell family eventually made their way to Nova Scotia.

Captain Crowell and his family were among the tens of thousands of United Empire Loyalists who arrived in British North America. Frightened and persecuted, they sought a new, safe homeland. Since then, Canada has built itself on the arrival of those, like the Loyalists, who have sought a new life and brought their valuable talents and gifts with them.

After America declared its independence in 1776, more than 100,000 settlers who remained loyal to the Crown—the origin of the name "Loyalists"—left the 13 colonies that had become the United States, where they were no longer welcome, to return to England or to settle in other British colonies.

In 1783, some 8,000 of these Loyalists sought refuge in Québec; another 35,600 fled to Nova Scotia. At the time the combined population of Québec and Nova Scotia was 166,000, with Québec accounting for 113,000. The Loyalists transformed the demographic makeup of British North America, especially in the colony of Nova Scotia. The majority of Loyalists who migrated to Canada were English speakers.

The authorities in the province of Québec and the colony of Nova Scotia granted these refugees between 200 and 1,200 acres of land for each family, as well as farm implements and sufficient food and clothing for two years.

Most of the Loyalists settled in Nova Scotia, lured by the economic potential of the colony, its British common-law system, and the fact that it was English-speaking. At the time, Nova Scotia also comprised the territory of present-day New Brunswick, but not St. John Island (now Prince Edward Island), which had been a separate colony since 1769. Before the arrival of the approximately 35,000 Loyalists, about 12,000 people of British origin inhabited the colony.

Among the new arrivals were 3,500 Black Loyalists, former slaves who had been freed or who belonged to wealthy White Loyalists or disbanded soldiers. Black Loyalist settlements in Nova Scotia were established in Annapolis Royal, in the area of Cornwallis/Horton, as well as in Weymouth, Digby, Windsor, Preston, Sydney, Parrsboro, Halifax, Shelburne, and Birchtown.

In 1994, Nova Scotia's Black Loyalist Heritage Society applied to the National Historic Sites and Monuments Board to have the landing of the Black Loyalists in Canada recognized as an event of national historic importance. The National Historic Sites and Monuments approved the application and honoured the Black Loyalists by creating a park and unveiling a monument in their memory in Birchtown, Shelburne County, Nova Scotia, on July 20, 1996.

The story of Nova Scotia's Black Loyalists was popularized by *The Book of Negroes*, a 2007 award-winning novel by Canadian author Lawrence Hill. In the United States, Australia and New Zealand, the novel was published under the title *Someone Knows My Name*.

Traces of the Loyalists and their significant contribution to the province are still evident. For example, journalist and writer Joseph Howe, one of Nova Scotia's greatest and best-loved politicians, is a Nova Scotia legend. Howe's father, John, was a United Empire Loyalist or "His Majesty's Yankee." The Howe family hailed from Massachusetts. Having remained loyal to the crown during the American Revolution, the family joined the flood of United Empire Loyalists out of the United States after the war. John Howe arrived in Halifax in 1779 and set up a printing shop, where he published the first issue of the *Halifax Journal* in December 1780. In 1798, he married Mary Edes; their son Joseph was born in Halifax on December 13, 1804. In 1828, Joseph Howe went into the printing business with the purchase of the *Novascotian*, a Halifax newspaper. Acting as its editor until 1841, Howe turned it into the province's most influential paper.

In 1835, after the *Novascotian* published a letter attacking Halifax politicians and police for pocketing public money, Howe was charged with seditious libel, a serious criminal offence. For more than six hours, Howe addressed the jury, citing countless examples of civic corruption. Moved by his passionate address, jurors acquitted him in what is now considered a landmark case for a free press in Canada. The following year, Howe was elected to the Legislative Assembly and, as a reformer, was instrumental in helping Nova Scotia become the first British colony to win responsible government in 1848. He served as premier of Nova Scotia from 1860 to 1863 and then joined the federal cabinet of Canada's first prime minister, Sir John A. Macdonald, in 1869. In 1873, Howe became the third lieutenant-governor of Nova Scotia. He died after less than one month in office.

In Windsor, Nova Scotia, the life of Loyalist and Scotswoman Flora MacDonald is commemorated at the Fort Edward National Historic Site. Built in 1750 to secure the overland route between Annapolis Royal, the old capital of Nova Scotia, and the new capital of Halifax, MacDonald spent one winter at the fort.

During the American Revolution, the fort was garrisoned to

protect the area from attack by American raiders. One of the captains of the British regiment occupying the fort was MacDonald's husband, Allan MacDonald. In 1774, Flora MacDonald and her husband left Scotland and immigrated to North Carolina. During the American Revolution, Captain MacDonald served the British government in the 84th Regiment of Foot (Royal Highland Emigrants).

On February 27, 1776, the Loyalists were defeated by the patriot militia at Moore's Creek Bridge near Wilmington. Captain MacDonald was taken captive and held prisoner for two years until a prisoner exchange occurred in 1777. He was then sent to Fort Edward where he took command of the 84th Regiment of Foot, Second Battalion. After her husband was taken prisoner, Flora MacDonald remained in hiding while the American Patriots ravaged her family plantation and took all her possessions. Courageously, she secretly visited and comforted families whose men had also been captured or been killed. When her husband was released from prison during the fall of 1778, she reunited with him at Fort Edward. Flora MacDonald, who had won fame as the rescuer of Bonnie Prince Charlie following the defeat of his Highland forces at the bloody Battle of Culloden in 1746, spent the winter of 1778-1779 at Fort Edward before she returned to Scotland.

A few years after MacDonald left Nova Scotia to return to Scotland, Porter's Lake, a community not far from where my grandfather lived most of his life, was settled by United Empire Loyalists and disbanded soldiers from the American Revolution. The tiny community was named after William Porter, a United Empire Loyalist, who along with others received a 1,650-acre grant of land that year, according to Lena Ferguson's *History of Porter's Lake: A Little Breezy Place*. Porter had arrived in Nova Scotia on the ship *Peace* after serving as Deputy Commissary General of Musters to the Foreign Troops of His Majesty. The Commissary General of Musters Office comprised the household troops, the cavalry, guards, and regular infantry regiments, as well as special regiments or corps, colonial troops, and various foreign legions and troops. In Nova Scotia, he established himself at the lower end of Porter's Lake, where the waters flow into Three Fathom Harbour, the tiny community where my grandfather spent his childhood. Porter built a sawmill by the lake and operated it until his death in 1800.

More than 230 years after my Loyalist ancestors arrived in Canada, I maintain a strong connection to our proud roots. I am a member of the United Empire Loyalists' Association of Canada and often attend Loyalist gatherings. Nova Scotia does not have a celebratory United Empire Loyalist Day like Ontario, but the Loyalist influence on the evolution of the province is still evident.

A Loyalist plaque has been placed in the Halifax Public Gardens, a beautiful 16-acre oasis in the heart of the city. Meant to honour the Loyalists and their descendants, the plaque is by the fountain which commemorates the Boer War. The plaque reminds me how blessed I am to live in such a marvellous country like Canada. My country did not just appear like a mountain out of the fog. Like any mountain, it took years to form. The American Revolution provided Canada with, among other things, the Loyalists. These people went on to defend and protect Canada in the War of 1812, fighting proudly among other Canadians. We owe them our freedom.

Epilogue

My wife, Florence, and I often stroll along Halifax's historic waterfront in the summer. One sunny day, about a decade ago, I felt a tap on my back as we passed the Maritime Museum of the Atlantic. I turned in surprise, expecting to see a familiar face, but no one was there. Seeing the confused look on my face, Florence asked me if I was okay. I explained what had happened. After some discussion we agreed that it must have been a sign from my grandfather. The presence I felt that day was so strong, I couldn't ignore it. He was urging me to bring his story to light again, this time to a wider audience.

I made a solemn promise to my grandparents that they would not be forgotten. Now that both are dead, I am sometimes lonely knowing that, as their only grandchild, I am the only one left who can help narrate the joys, sorrows, and adventures that made up their lives.

Long ago, an old man, his dog, and his grandson stood on a wooden pier in Dartmouth watching the ships leaving the Bedford Basin. The boy looked at his grandfather and wondered what memories visited him and brought a wistful look to his eyes. As a sailing ship passed the pier heading to the open ocean, the man and the boy admired her deck of long planks of solid teak running fore and aft, the rows of belaying pins standing along the sides, the high head of the forecastle, and her canvas sails blowing on the wind.

The boy joined his grandfather in imagining sailing adventures in the faraway Spice Islands of Indonesia, Mandalay, and Tahiti. The boy would later realize that his grandfather's sailing stories didn't have to die with him. If he wanted to save them, he could. And he did.

Frank Crowell Leaman holding his grandfather's model of the *Queen Mary*.

ACKNOWLEDGEMENTS

I would like to thank the Maritime Museum of the Atlantic, Nova Scotia Archives, Dalhousie University, Halifax Public Libraries, Fisheries Museum of the Atlantic, Dartmouth Heritage Museum, Age of Sail Heritage Museum (Port Greville, NS), United Empire Loyalists' Association, British Consulate, Frank and Heather Johnson, Capt. Robert Cormier, Valerie Lenethen, Dan Conlin, Allison Lawlor, Dennis Macormick, Geoff Frampton, Gavin Will, Stephanie Porter, Iona Bulgin, and, as usual, those I have forgotten.

—*Frank Crowell Leaman*

NOTES ON THE TEXT

The Roar of the Sea, as told by Capt. William Arthur Crowell, was transcribed by his grandson, Frank Leaman, in the early 1950s. Several copies of the book were printed at a hardware store in downtown Dartmouth; most were passed along to family members.

The original text has been edited by writer Allison Lawlor to correct misspellings and repetition and to improve readability. Geographical references have been added for ease of reading.

Capt. Crowell loved poetry and hymns; he copied excerpts from sailor's poetry and other poems and hymns he encountered. These were included in the original *Roar of the Sea*, and some have been preserved in this reprint, though their origins are not always known.

Leaman's memories and reflections, as well as the family's Loyalist history, were recorded by Lawlor in 2014 and added to the edited original manuscript. Most of the photos and newspaper clippings in this book were gathered over the years by the Crowell family and now reside in Leaman's personal collection.